THE KEYS TO SPIRITUAL GROWTH

THE

KEYS

TO

SPIRITUAL

GROWTH

UNLOCKING THE RICHES OF GOD

~

JOHN MACARTHUR

:: CROSSWAY®

WHEATON, ILLINOIS

The Keys to Spiritual Growth
Revised and expanded edition copyright © 1991 by John F. MacArthur, Jr.
Originally published by Fleming H. Revell Company, 1976.
Crossway first edition published 2001

Published by Crossway
    1300 Crescent Street
    Wheaton, Illinois 60187

Unless otherwise identified, Scripture quotations are from the *New American Standard Bible,* © The Lockman Foundation, 1960, 1962, 1963, 1968, 1971, 1972, 1973, 1975, 1977, 1995.

Scripture quotations identified KJV are from the *King James Version* of the Bible.

"The Fizzie Principle" is reprinted from *Found: God's Will* by John F. MacArthur, Jr., published by Victor Books, copyright © 1973, revised 1977, by SP Publications, Inc., Wheaton, Illinois 60187

Quotation from *Peanuts* reprinted by permission of United Feature Syndicate, Inc.

Cover design: Cindy Kiple

First Crossway printing, 2001

Printed in the United States of America

ISBN-13: 978-1-58134-269-7
ISBN-10: 1-58134-269-1
epub ISBN: 978-1-4335-1741-9
PDF ISBN: 978-1-4335-1085-4
Mobipocket ISBN: 978-1-4335-1084-7

Library of Congress Cataloging-in-Publication Data
MacArthur, John, 1939-
    The keys to spiritual growth : unlocking the riches of God / John F.
MacArthur.—Rev. and expanded.
      p.   cm.
    Includes biographical references and index.
    ISBN 13: 978-1-58134-269-7
    ISBN 10: 1-58134-269-1 (TPB : alk. paper)
    1. Christian life. 2. Spiritual life—Christianity. I. Title.
BB4501.3.M23   2001
248.4—dc21   2001001181

Crossway is a publishing ministry of Good News Publishers.
CH   27   26   25   24   23   22   21   20

To
Matthew, Marcy, Mark and Melinda

*my beloved children, whose spiritual growth
is my constant concern and whose maturity
will be my highest earthly joy*

Until we all attain to the unity of the faith, and of the knowledge of the Son of God, to a mature man, to the measure of the stature which belongs to the fullness of Christ. As a result, we are no longer to be children, tossed here and there by waves and carried about by every wind of doctrine, by the trickery of men, by craftiness in deceitful scheming; but speaking the truth in love, we are to grow up in all aspects into Him who is the head, even Christ.

Ephesians 4:13-15

Grow in the grace and knowledge of our Lord and Savior Jesus Christ. To Him be the glory, both now and to the day of eternity. Amen.

2 Peter 3:18

CONTENTS

ACKNOWLEDGMENTS

Thanks to Dr. Lowell Saunders, who edited the first edition of this book many years ago. Thanks also to Dave Enos, Allacin Morimizu, and Phil Johnson, who helped with this revision.

INTRODUCTION

We don't hear much about spiritual growth these days. Many Christians in our society have been diverted by various teachings that promise power, spiritual energy, and success without the process of growth into spiritual maturity. They look for dramatic experiences, climactic turning points, instant solutions to their spiritual problems; but real, lasting victory doesn't come through those means. God's design is that we be seasoned to maturity through a continual process of growth.

The contemporary church's de-emphasis of spiritual growth has reaped a bitter harvest. Millions of professing Christians suffer from arrested development. Churches are filled with people who are spiritually immature, undiscerning, weak, and fragile. Spiritual underdevelopment is the rule, no longer an exception. Thousands—perhaps millions—are now addicted to "therapy," evidently preferring the dependency of a counseling relationship to the rigors of true discipleship and growth in grace.

This is a severe threat to the church. Frankly, it may be a sign that something is terribly wrong, for growth is one of the essential signs of life—in both the physical and the spiritual realms. Where there is no growth, no true life exists. Where there is no spiritual growth, there is good reason to question whether spiritual life exists.

Are you growing? If you are not, or if you are not satisfied with your rate of growth, this book is for you!

Be sure of this: God intends every Christian to grow into spiritual maturity. His Word commands us, "Grow in the grace and knowledge of our Lord and Savior Jesus Christ" (2 Peter 3:18). That's our obligation—and our privilege. Each day we can progress in our spiritual life toward a fuller, higher, personal, experiential knowledge of God and Christ. We can go past His Word to the God who wrote it and know Him more personally.

I find that many people entertain mistaken ideas about what spiritual maturity involves. They're not growing as rapidly as they could, or they're caught on a level far below where they should be, because they misunderstand what spiritual maturity is and how one grows in grace. Here are a few reminders to help keep us on track.

Spiritual growth has nothing to do with our position in Christ. God sees us in His Son as already perfect. We are complete in Him (Colossians 2:10). We have everything we need pertaining to life and godliness (2 Peter 1:3). We are new creations (2 Corinthians 5:17). Positionally we are perfect. Practically, however, we fall far short. Growth is the process by which that which is true of us positionally becomes more and more a reality in practice as well.

Spiritual growth has nothing to do with God's favor. God doesn't like us better the more spiritual we become. Sometimes parents threaten their children, "If you don't behave, the Lord won't like you." How ridiculous! God's love for us is not conditional upon our behavior. Even when we were "helpless," "ungodly," "sinners," and "enemies" (see Romans 5:6-10), God showed His great love for us by sending His Son to die for our sins. God cannot love us more just because we grow.

Spiritual growth has nothing to do with time. Maturity in the spiritual realm is not measured by the calendar. It is possible for a person to be a Christian for half a century and yet remain a spiritual infant. Several years ago I saw a report in *Time* magazine about a Bible quiz given to high-school students. According to the students, Sodom and Gomorrah were lovers; the Gospels were written by Matthew, Mark, Luther, and John; Eve was created from an apple; and Jezebel was Ahab's jackass! Don't think those high-school students were unusual. I know some retired persons who might do even worse!

Spiritual growth has nothing to do with knowledge. Facts, data, information, and intelligence cannot be equated with spiritual maturity. You might score perfectly on *Time* magazine's quiz, but unless your knowledge results in conforming you to Christ, it is useless. Truth that fails to change your life and behavior may in fact be hurtful, hardening you instead of bringing you to maturity.

Spiritual growth has nothing to do with activity. Some people make the mistake of assuming that the most mature Christians are always the busiest ones. But busyness doesn't necessarily bring maturity, nor can it be substituted for maturity. Excessive activity may, in fact, even hinder what is really vital and important in the Christian life. Matthew 7:21-23 tells us of a group who will plead acceptance with Christ on the basis of their many wonderful works, but He will cast them out. Busyness can't earn salvation, let alone bring about spiritual maturity.

Spiritual growth has nothing to do with prosperity. "Well, look how the Lord has blessed me," some people exclaim. "I have so much money, and I have a wonderful house and a nice car and a secure job. See how God has blessed me because I've honored Him?" Don't believe it. God may have allowed you to prosper, but that is not a mark of spiritual growth. (See 2 Corinthians 12:7-10.) Some people so dedicate themselves to the pursuit of prosperity that they neglect everything else. That is not spiritual maturity, but just the opposite.

Spiritual growth, as we have noted, is simply matching up our practice with our position. Our position in Christ is majestic. God has "raised us up with Him, and seated us with Him in the heavenly places in Christ Jesus" (Ephesians 2:6). Our position could not be more lofty. Positionally, we are perfect. Now God wants us to reflect that position in our progressive experience. That's what growth is all about.

Spiritual growth is critical. Call it what you will: pursuing righteousness (1 Timothy 6:11), being transformed (Romans 12:2), "perfecting holiness" (2 Corinthians 7:1), pressing toward the goal (Philippians 3:14), or being built up in the faith (Colossians 2:7). The goal is the same for every Christian: to be ". . . transformed into [the Lord's] image . . ." (2 Corinthians 3:18).

Spiritual growth is not mystical, sentimental, devotional, psychological, or the result of clever secrets. It comes through understanding and practicing the principles that are given in the Word of God. Its boundless blessings are in a divine vault that is easily unlocked by a series of unique keys. Those keys are the theme of this book. Get ready to unlock the riches of God in Christ Jesus!

1

THE
MASTER KEY

A Presupposition

The Bible is alive: "The word of God is living and active and sharper than any two-edged sword, and piercing as far as the division of soul and spirit, of both joints and marrow, and able to judge the thoughts and intentions of the heart" (Hebrews 4:12). Peter speaks of God's Word as that which is "imperishable . . . living and enduring" (1 Peter 1:23). Paul refers to the Bible as "the word of life" (Philippians 2:16).

THE BIBLE'S VITAL SIGNS
In what sense does the Word of God live? We can best see that by comparing it with the decay, destruction, and corruption that surround us. Death is the monarch of this world. This earth is nothing but a large cemetery; everyone is dying. Some people think they are living it up. Actually, they're living on the downside, for their bodies and their glory soon wither and fade away like the grass (1 Peter 1:24).

In contrast, the Bible is inexhaustible, inextinguishable, and life-giving. The death and decay of the world system cannot touch it.

The Bible is alive in itself. The Bible is perennially fresh. In every generation and every age, the Bible proves itself to be alive and relevant. Its riches are inexhaustible, its depths unfathomable.

A few years ago I decided to choose a book of the Bible and read that same book every day for thirty days. I figured at the end of a month I would really know that particular book. I started with a relatively short book—1 John. At the end of thirty days, I discovered there were still things that I did not know about the book; so I read it for another month. Even after that I felt I didn't know 1 John as well as I wanted to; so I read it for another thirty days. Do you know something? First John still holds mysteries for me that I haven't even tapped. Every time I read it, I get excited!

Another reason we say the Bible lives is that it is up-to-date. Have you ever looked at your old high school or college textbooks? Most of them are obsolete. The march of progress and discovery has left them behind. But the Bible speaks as perceptively and definitively to the twenty-first century as it did to the first century.

The Bible discerns hearts. It has insight that shakes us up. It is a sharp, two-edged sword that dissects our innermost beings. It judges the thoughts and intentions of our hearts (Hebrews 4:12). It reveals to us exactly what we are, which is why those who cling to their sin don't read it—they don't want to be convicted. Those are some of the reasons we say the Word of God is alive.

The Bible is life-giving. The Bible not only *has* life—it also *gives* life. The power to reproduce is a fundamental characteristic of life. Mere human thoughts and words cannot impart spiritual life. But the living Word of God can. James 1:18 says, "In the exercise of His will He brought us forth by the word of truth." The Holy Spirit uses the Word to bring about new birth. The only way to become a child of God is through the living Word: "So faith comes from hearing, and hearing by the word of Christ" (Romans 10:17). We are "born again not of seed which is perishable but imperishable, that is, through the living and enduring word of God" (1 Peter 1:23).

Consider the parable of the sower in Luke 8. The Word of God is the seed scattered over the world (v. 11). Some falls by the wayside and is snatched away by the devil so people won't believe and be saved. What is the germ of life that people must believe to be saved? The life-giving Word.

Jesus stressed the importance of the Word in the process of regeneration. "It is the Spirit who gives life; the flesh profits nothing; the words that I have spoken to you are spirit and are life" (John 6:63). The Spirit of God uses the Word of God to produce life.

The Bible sustains spiritual life. As the Puritan Thomas Watson said, Scripture is both the breeder and the feeder of life. By it we are spiritually born, and by it we are nourished to maturity. Peter said, "Like newborn babes, long for the pure milk of the word, so that by it you may grow in respect to salvation" (1 Peter 2:2).

Have you ever seen a hungry newborn baby? That baby isn't interested in hearing you talk, in playing with you, or being cuddled. Nothing short of being fed will satisfy. Peter tells us that our desire for the Word should be that strong.

Many Christians do not strongly desire the Word. As a result they are emaciated and improperly nourished, suffering from spiritual malnutrition. They need to remember the words of Jeremiah, "Your words were found and I ate them, and Your words became for me a joy and the delight of my heart" (Jeremiah 15:16).

Paul reminded Timothy of that truth: "In pointing out these things to the brethren, you will be a good servant of Christ Jesus, constantly nourished on the words of the faith and of the sound doctrine which you have been following" (1 Timothy 4:6).

The Word of God nourishes believers. We need it just as a baby needs milk, but we also need to grow up so we can take in solid food (Hebrews 5:13, 14).

The Bible transforms lives. Paul encouraged the Ephesians to be renewed in the spirit of their minds (Ephesians 4:23). In Romans 12:2 he said that the renewing of our minds transforms us. Even as believers, we need to let the Word change us. We do not become perfect when we become believers. The Holy Spirit still has a lot to do to mold us into Christlikeness. We still struggle with our old sinful patterns of living (see Romans 7:15-25). Only through filling our minds with the Word and living in obedience to its principles can those patterns be changed.

Many Christians struggle with the problem of how to be more committed to the Lord. They attend seminars, read books, seek certain spiritual gifts, see counselors, listen to talk shows—just about everything except turning to the Bible. Yet if they neglect the Word, little if any change will result. Only the Holy Spirit, working through the Word, has the power to bring us to maturity in Christ.

Paul reminded the Corinthians of that truth: "But we all, with unveiled face, beholding as in a mirror the glory of the Lord, are being transformed into the same image from glory to glory, just as from the Lord, the Spirit" (2 Corinthians 3:18). What is the "mirror" he speaks of? Scripture. James wrote, "If anyone is a hearer of the word and not a doer, he is like a man who looks at his natural face in a mirror; for once he has looked at himself and gone away, he has immediately forgotten what kind of person he was" (James 1:23, 24). How do we become transformed to be like Christ? As we see the glory of Jesus Christ revealed in the mirror of Scripture, the Spirit of God transforms us into the image of Jesus Christ. That is the master key to spiritual growth.

The Puritan Philip Henry wrote:

> Conversion turns us to the Word of God, as our touchstone, to examine ourselves . . . as our glass, to dress by (James 1); as our rule to walk and work by (Galatians 6:16); as our water, to wash us (Psalm 119:9); as our fire to warm us (Luke 24); as our food to nourish us (Job 23:12); as our sword to fight with (Ephesians 6); as our counselor, in all our doubts (Psalm 119:24); as our cordial, to comfort us; as our heritage, to enrich us.

THERE ARE NO SHORTCUTS TO SPIRITUAL MATURITY

Many Christians try to figure out some kind of shortcut to spiritual maturity, but none exists. As we gaze into the mirror of the Word of God and behold the glory of God, as we allow the sword of the Spirit to do surgery on our souls, as we permit the water of the Word to cleanse us, the Holy Spirit will transform our lives.

The most significant step in my personal spiritual development took place when I committed myself to intense study of the Bible. Bible study has become the passion of my life. Nothing in this world consumes me like the desire to study and communicate the

Word. While I haven't arrived at the goal of perfect Christlikeness (Philippians 3:13, 14), I have learned that the Holy Spirit uses the Word to transform me into the image of Christ.

The Bible is central to our spiritual lives. It is instrumental in our regeneration and crucial to our spiritual growth. In it God "has granted to us everything pertaining to life and godliness" (2 Peter 1:3). And we pay a high price for neglecting it.

USING THE MASTER KEY

Let me suggest five specific ways to use the master key of spiritual growth—the Word of God.

Believe It

Today many voices compete with the Scriptures for our allegiance. Science, psychology, humanism, and mysticism are all rival sources of authority to the Bible, clamoring loudly for our attention. Don't follow the majority. Too many in the church seem willing to abandon God's Word for supposed shortcuts to maturity. But Peter's response must be ours: "Lord, to whom shall we go? You have words of eternal life" (John 6:68). Accept the Bible for what it is—the divinely inspired, infallible, inerrant, all-sufficient Word of God. Doubting the truths God has revealed in Scripture will rob us of our joy and may ultimately destroy our faith altogether.[1]

Study It

All Christians should make it their goal to be, like Apollos, "mighty in the Scriptures" (Acts 18:24). Too many Christians are content with shallow, superficial Bible study or even no Bible study at all. Such neglect of serious study can result in doctrinal error as well as misconceptions on how to live the Christian life. The Bible rewards diligent study. And through study of the Scriptures, we can show ourselves approved of God (2 Timothy 2:15).

Honor It

The citizens of Ephesus honored the statue of Diana because they thought Jupiter had sent it down from heaven. So they worshiped it—ugly, obscene, and horrible as it was. But something of true beauty has come down out of heaven from God—His precious Word, which is more valuable than gold or jewels (Proverbs 3:14, 15). Don't pay lip service to the Bible while in reality you give your life in pursuit of the world's substitutes—including things like entertainment, politics, philosophy, psychology, mysticism, and personal experience.

Love It

"O how I love Your law! It is my meditation all the day," wrote the psalmist (119:97). Can you say that? Do you give the Word as much of your time and attention as you do other, less-deserving objects of affection? Do you read the Bible as a love letter sent to you from God? Is the Word of God your passion, something to which you are drawn in quiet moments, or do you turn instead to diversions that actually hinder your growth?

Obey It

Obedience is ultimately the only appropriate response to God's Word. It will do us no good to believe, study, honor, and love the Bible unless we also obey it. The commands of God aren't optional; they are obligatory. We can't approach the Bible like a smorgasbord, whimsically choosing what we wish to obey and bypassing the rest. Our obedience must be implicit. Samuel told the disobedient Saul, "Has the LORD as much delight in burnt offerings and sacrifices as in obeying the voice of the LORD? Behold, to obey is better than sacrifice, and to heed than the fat of rams" (1 Samuel 15:22).

So you will find God's Word to be a master key that opens everything else in the spiritual realm! No chamber of spiritual privilege is closed to this key. Despite what many believe and teach today, nothing apart from the Word—no spiritual experience, no mystical key, no supernatural secret, no transcendental formula—can unlock the way to some spiritual power unavailable through Scripture.

Certainly there are other keys, each unlocking a unique, treasured principle of spiritual growth. But they are all based on this one great master key: Each one is a principle from the Word.

The great revival of Nehemiah's day began when the people urged him to read the Scriptures to them (Nehemiah 8). As they listened, their hearts were awakened. They were convicted, cleansed, built up—and they responded in obedience.

Perhaps you are hungry for personal revival. I urge you to allow the Word of God to be the key that will unlock for you the vast repository of spiritual riches that are yours in Christ.

2

THE
MASTER PURPOSE

The Glory of God

If you were to go out on the street and ask ten people at random to name what they considered to be the greatest theme in all the world, you would probably get a variety of answers: money, love, marriage, sex, freedom, security, status, pleasure, peace, happiness.

But from God's viewpoint, there is only one answer. It is the greatest theme in all the universe. It is the purpose of creation, the primary goal of the Christian life, and the reason for everything God has done or will do.

What is it? The answer is found in the *Westminster Shorter Catechism*. The first question asks, "What is the chief end of man?" And here's the answer: "The chief end of man is to glorify God and to enjoy Him forever." The writers of the catechism believed every Christian should understand that he exists for God's glory and God is for his enjoyment.

Someone may object that we are basing too much on the catechism, even though it is based on Scripture. But the paramount importance of the glory of God is not just someone's idea. It is supported directly by the Word of God. In Psalm 16:8 David writes, "I have set the LORD continually before me." That refers to giving God glory. In making this statement David is saying in effect, "In everything I do, my attention is given to God. All that I do, I accomplish with my focus riveted on God. It's all for His glory and His honor and His will."

The result of such a focus is found in verse 9: "Therefore my heart is glad and my glory rejoices." That is another way of saying that he found great joy in God. So here was David's goal—to live always to the glory of God and consequently to enjoy God forever. That is the same point that the catechism is making.

The supreme objective in the life of any man or woman should be to give God glory. And the consequence of doing that will be unbounded joy. Spiritual maturity comes from concentrating on the person of God until one is caught up and lost in His majesty.

GOD'S INTRINSIC GLORY

What do we mean by *glorifying* God? We can look at this practically from two aspects. The first concerns God's intrinsic glory, the glory that God has in Himself. In Isaiah 6:3, the seraphim cried out, "Holy, Holy, Holy, is the Lord of hosts, the whole earth is full of His glory."

God's intrinsic glory is a part of His being. It is not something that was given to Him. If men and angels had never been created, God would still possess His intrinsic glory. If no one ever gave Him any glory, any honor, or any praise, He would still be the glorious God that He is. That is intrinsic glory—the glory of God's nature. It is the manifestation and combination of all His attributes. We cannot give it to Him; we cannot diminish it. He is who He is—"the God of glory" (Acts 7:2).

Human glory is quite unlike that—it is not intrinsic; rather, it is imparted to a person from outside his or her essential being. We speak of people being exalted and honored. But if you take off a king's robes and crown and put him next to a beggar, you wouldn't be able to tell them apart. The only glory a human ruler enjoys is that which is given him by the trappings of his office.

All of God's glory is part of His essential being. It is not granted to Him, nor does it derive from any source outside of Himself. So the glory God possesses is thus very different from any form of human glory.

In addition to various Old Testament references, such as Psalm 24:7-10, the New Testament also teaches that God is a God of glory. The Gospels tell us that during His earthly life, the Lord Jesus Christ was divine glory incarnate (John 1:14).

The raising of Lazarus illustrates the Savior's glory. When Jesus ordered the removal of the stone that sealed Lazarus' grave, Martha protested. But Jesus answered, "Did I not say to you that if you believe, you will see the glory of God?" (John 11:40).

How was God's glory displayed in that instance? In the manifestation of His power—the same power He used to create the universe. Martha did not give the Lord Jesus that glory; He already had it. In raising Lazarus, He put it on display.

Jesus later prayed, "Father, I desire that they also, whom You have given Me, be with Me where I am, so that they may see My glory which You have given Me" (John 17:24). The answer to that prayer will be realized in the time described in Revelation 21:23. The New Jerusalem will have no need of sun or moon, "for the glory of God has illumined it, and its lamp is the Lamb." How beautifully that shows God's glory as an essential, intrinsic part of His very nature! Since the glory of God is part of His essential being, it is something He does not give to anyone else. In Isaiah 48:11 He says, "My glory I will not give to another." God never divests Himself of His glory.

But believers can *reflect* God's glory, as Moses did when he came down from the mountain (Exodus 34:30-35). More than that, God's glory shines from within every Christian (2 Corinthians 3:18). But God never imparts His glory to anyone apart from Himself. That is, His glory is in believers only because He Himself indwells them. The glory never becomes ours; God never divests Himself of His glory.

This is similar to the relationship between Pharaoh and Joseph in Genesis. Pharaoh gave Joseph his ring, symbolizing royal authority. He also gave him a gold chain (Genesis 41:42). Joseph became Pharaoh's representative, with full imperial privileges. Joseph essentially ruled Egypt. His word was law. But there was one thing Pharaoh did not give up—his glory. He told Joseph, "Only in the throne I will be greater than you" (v. 40). He did not give up his glory.

Likewise, God's glory is something that He does not share with any created being. It is intrinsic to Him—the sum of His attributes. It cannot be added to or diminished.

MAGNIFYING GOD'S GLORY BEFORE OTHERS

You might ask, if God's glory cannot be added to or increased in any way, why do we speak of bringing glory to God? How can one give God glory if God's glory is absolute and intrinsic?

Actually, when we speak of glorifying God, we're talking about magnifying God's glory before the world. We can, of course, add nothing to the glory that is His very essence, but we can reflect and amplify God's glory to others.

That was Paul's point in Titus 2:10, where he wrote that Christians should seek to "adorn the doctrine of God our Savior in every respect." That verse is not speaking of adding anything to God's attributes. By living a holy life, we affect the testimony about God in the world. We don't adorn God; we adorn the doctrine, or teaching, about God by allowing people to see His glory reflected in the way we live. Jesus told His disciples to live so that people can "see your good works, and glorify your Father who is in heaven" (Matthew 5:16). So while we cannot add anything to God's intrinsic glory, our lives can reflect His glory and magnify it in other people's comprehension. That's how we bring glory to God.

We can also give God glory through spoken testimony. In 1 Chronicles 16:24 David says, "Tell of His glory among the nations, His wonderful deeds among all the peoples." When we declare the great things God has done in our lives, He is glorified.

We also give God glory when we praise Him. David said of God, "Yours, O LORD, is the greatness and the power and the glory and the victory and the majesty, indeed everything that is in the heavens and the earth; Yours is the dominion, O LORD, and You exalt Yourself as head over all" (1 Chronicles 29:11). After making that declaration, David summed up: "Now therefore, our God, we thank You, and praise Your glorious name" (v. 13). David recognized that God possessed intrinsic glory and that He ought to be praised because of it.

The New Testament also speaks of praising God for His glory. Paul does so in 1 Timothy 1:17: "Now to the King eternal, immortal, invisible, the only God, be honor and glory forever and ever. Amen." At the end of his epistle, Paul praises God for being the One "who alone possesses immortality and dwells in unapproachable light, whom no man has seen or can see. To Him be honor and eternal dominion! Amen" (6:16).

Jude echoes that same theme: "To the only God our Savior . . . be glory, majesty, dominion and authority, before all time and now and forever. Amen" (Jude 25). And in Revelation we find great hosts of people proclaiming God's glory (5:13). The New Testament commands us to lead lives that glorify God. Paul prayed that "Christ will even now, as always, be exalted in my body" (Philippians 1:20). He desired to exalt Christ in the eyes of the world. He exhorted the Corinthians to "glorify God in your body" (1 Corinthians 6:20). In other words, use your body in such a way as to give glory to God. Finally, Paul gave this all-inclusive command in 1 Corinthians 10:31: "Whether, then, you eat or drink or whatever you do, do all to the glory of God." Everything we do, even something as mundane as eating and drinking, is to be done to glorify God.

GOD'S GLORY THROUGH THE AGES

God's plan for the ages involves successive manifestations of His glory. History is the unfolding of God's glory in the past. Prophecy foretells the future revelation of its fullness. And the church is the arena where God has chosen uniquely to display His glory in the present.

Creation

The created universe silently witnesses to the glory of its Creator. The psalmist writes, "The heavens are telling of the glory of God;

and their expanse is declaring the work of His hands" (Psalm 19:1). Isaiah informs us, "The whole earth is full of His glory" (6:3). Even the animal world glorifies its Creator (Isaiah 43:20).

Did you ever wonder why God created the universe? Colossians 1:16 gives the answer: "For by Him all things were created, both in the heavens and on earth, visible and invisible, whether thrones or dominions or rulers or authorities—all things have been created through Him and for Him." The universe was created to bring glory to God.

Everything in the universe, from the smallest subatomic particles to the biggest stars, gives Him glory, with two exceptions—fallen angels and fallen men. Since the purpose of everything is to give God glory, that which doesn't is cast from His presence. Hence fallen angels and unredeemed men will spend eternity away from the presence of God. Although God takes no pleasure in such punishment (Ezekiel 33:11), it nevertheless brings Him glory by revealing His holiness.

The Garden of Eden

In the Garden of Eden, God manifested His glory to Adam and Eve. Genesis 3:8 tells us that they heard the voice of the Lord walking in the Garden in the cool of the day. But this same verse also tells us that, in an effort to escape responsibility for their sin, they attempted to hide from the presence of the Lord. So it is evident that God came to them not only through a voice but in some visible manifestation of His glory, possibly a brilliant shining light (compare Exodus 13:21; Acts 9:3-6).

What a fantastic privilege Adam and Eve enjoyed, to see God's glory manifested daily! How long they continued to enjoy that sight, no one knows. But the day came when they rebelled against God. Their sin rendered them unfit to be in the same place where His glory was. So God cast them out of the Garden. He punctuated their expulsion by stationing cherubim (angelic beings whose task is guarding the holiness of God) at the Garden entrance, to prevent them from returning to the Garden. A flaming sword turned every direction to cut off access to the tree of life (Genesis 3:24). The principle revealed in that account holds true today. Sinful, fallen men cannot stand in God's presence.

Adam and Eve lived the rest of their lives with that sword blocking any hope they might have had of reentering the Garden. It cut them off from further face-to-face communion with God. The sword spoke of judgment—a judgment of death for sin. Someone had to pay that awful, eternal penalty so that the human race could once again have communion with God. On whom did the judgment fall? "For Christ also died for sins once for all, the just for the unjust, so that He might bring us to God" (1 Peter 3:18). Christ's death satisfied the demands of God's justice, and because of that, those who place their faith in Him can regain fellowship and communion with God.

Moses

God next chose to manifest His glory to Moses. Moses was a very humble man (Numbers 12:3) with a modest view of his own capabilities. When God called him to be His prophet and to lead His people, Moses tried to get out of it, arguing that he was not an eloquent speaker (Exodus 4:10). The Lord replied, "Who has made man's mouth? . . . Now then go, and I, even I, will be with your mouth, and teach you what you are to say" (vv. 11, 12). But Moses still objected, until finally the Lord assigned Aaron to be his spokesman. In spite of Moses' hesitancy, God used him to reveal His glory to Israel (Exodus 33, 34).

Moses assumed his role as the leader of God's people. Israel left Egypt and traveled to Mount Sinai under Moses' leadership. God directed their path and miraculously preserved them from the Egyptian army, from the waters of the Red Sea, and from thirst and starvation. The Exodus was one of the most dramatic and remarkable displays of divine power the world has ever witnessed.

But while Moses was on Mount Sinai, receiving the Law from the hand of God, the people of Israel fell into gross sin (Exodus 32). Moses reminded the Lord that He had commissioned him to lead Israel to the Promised Land. Then he prayed, "If I have found favor in Your sight, let me know Your ways that I may know You"

(Exodus 33:13). Moses knew he couldn't make it on his own. God assured Moses that His presence would go with him (v. 14).

But Moses still wasn't satisfied and asked for a vision of God: "Show me Your glory!" (v. 18). Would God do it? How Moses must have strained to hear the reply: "I Myself will make all My goodness pass before you, and will proclaim the name of the LORD before you" (v. 19).

The word "goodness" there refers to the essence of God's glorious attributes, characterized by grace and mercy. The sum of God's attributes is so glorious that it is fatal for humans to look at! To stare unprotected at the full manifestation of God's glory would have meant instant death. God accordingly told Moses:

> *"You cannot see My face, for no man can see Me and live! . . .*
> *Behold there is a place by Me, and you shall stand there on the*
> *rock; and it will come about, while My glory is passing by, that*
> *I will put you in the cleft of the rock and cover you with My*
> *hand until I have passed by. Then I will take my hand away and*
> *you shall see My back, but My face shall not be seen."*
>
> —EXODUS 33:20-23

Does God have a face or a hand? Of course not. God is a "spirit" without physical form (John 4:24). Yet He often uses words referring to the body to allow us to understand in some measure what He is like. So when God speaks of His face or hand, He is accommodating Himself to our terminology.

Once precautions had been taken to protect Moses, God made good on His promise:

> *The LORD descended in the cloud and stood there with him as*
> *he called upon the name of the LORD. Then the LORD passed*
> *by in front of him and proclaimed, "The LORD, the LORD God,*
> *compassionate and gracious, slow to anger, and abounding in*
> *lovingkindness and truth; who keeps lovingkindness for thou-*
> *sands, who forgives iniquity, transgression and sin."*
>
> —EXODUS 34:5-7

Unlike many today who speak rather flippantly of their alleged encounters with God, Moses "made haste to bow low toward the earth and worship" (v. 8).

Reflected Glory and the Veil

What Moses saw was the *shekinah*—a visible manifestation of God's glory. What was the effect of it on Moses? Some of the afterglow rubbed off on him, and his face shone, although he was unaware of it (Exodus 34:29). In fact, his face shone so much that Aaron and the others were afraid to get anywhere near him (v. 30). Even the dim reflection of God's glory in Moses' face was an awe-inspiring sight.

When I was a young child, my parents took me to Knott's Berry Farm, which had a store that sold all kinds of items that glowed in the dark. I thought they were the greatest things I had ever seen. My parents told me to find something I liked, and they would buy it for me. So I selected a little figure and kept it in a bag for the rest of the day. When I got home that night, I took it out and put it on my dresser. It didn't glow, and I felt deeply disappointed.

"Do you know why it doesn't glow?" my father asked. "You have to hold it up to some other light. It doesn't have any of its own." So my dad held it next to a light bulb for a minute or so, and then I took it back to my darkened room. Now it worked beautifully!

Moses was something like that little fluorescent figure. He had no light of his own either. But after standing near the most brilliant light in the universe, he glowed. His face was charged with the glory of God. The Lord chose to send Moses off that mountaintop with a little of the glow of Deity. For a time Moses placed a veil over his face so the people could come near him. When Moses reentered the presence of God, he would remove the veil. Then he would speak to the Lord in open fellowship. The glory on Moses' face would be briefly renewed, and again he would veil his face when talking to the people (vv. 33-35).

Why did Moses wear the veil? Not because the reflected glory on his face posed a danger. Rather, the glow was gradually fading away, and he didn't want the people to be distracted by a fading kind of glory. That little figure I had sitting on top of my dresser didn't glow for more than an hour or so without some recharging from another light source. And that's what happened with Moses. The New Testament tells us that Moses did not want "the sons of Israel [to] look intently at the end of what was fading away" (2 Corinthians 3:13). Moses knew the glory was not his own. It was fading, and he didn't want his people to see the glory leave his face.

Twice in human history God had visibly manifested His glory— once in a place, once in a face. The people of Israel must have wondered if they would ever see such a manifestation again.

Glory in a Tent

God did display His glory visibly to Israel again—in the Tabernacle (a sort of temple in a tent), which was built to glorify God. God often chooses to use lowly, humble things to reveal His glory. That was certainly true of the Tabernacle. We often think of it as a pretty place, but in reality it was made of many weather-beaten, dull, unattractive animal skins staked out with tent poles. It was basically just a big, ugly, portable shelter. What made it special was what it symbolized: the God of Israel and His glory. It was the dwelling place of God's Spirit during the Israelites' journey from Egypt. Here God chose to manifest the *shekinah* to a whole nation.

God had given the Israelites detailed instructions about how to build the Tabernacle. When at last it was finished, "the cloud covered the tent of meeting, and the glory of the LORD filled the tabernacle. Moses was not able to enter the tent of meeting because the cloud had settled on it, and the glory of the LORD filled the tabernacle" (Exodus 40:34, 35). Picture the scene: The twelve tribes of Israel—perhaps several million people—lined up in order as God had positioned them. Right in the middle was the Tabernacle, with the glory of God filling it so that no one could enter.

Later, on the Day of Atonement, the high priest entered the Holy of Holies and stood before the ark of the covenant. You may think of the ark as beautiful, gleaming gold, but it was probably dulled and encrusted with the sacrificial blood the priests had sprinkled on it. The only beautiful thing about it would have been the wings of the cherubim stretched out over the mercy seat. Yet here God chose to visibly manifest His glory. Each time the high priest entered into that sacred place, he saw the glory of God.

In the Temple

For several hundred years God manifested His glory in the Tabernacle, but as in the Garden and on the face of Moses, this was only temporary. Eventually, during the reign of Solomon, the Tabernacle was replaced by the Temple. Just as God had given instructions concerning the building of the Tabernacle, so also He gave blueprints for the building of the Temple. Its purpose was to house the glory of God. It was a magnificent building, taking nearly eight years to build and probably costing the equivalent of several million dollars.

At last the day of dedication came, and what a day it was! "It happened that when the priests came from the holy place, the cloud filled the house of the LORD, so that the priests could not stand to minister because of the cloud, for the glory of the LORD filled the house of the LORD" (1 Kings 8:10, 11). Once again God in His condescending grace manifested His presence among His people.

Although the Temple was built as a permanent dwelling place for God's glory, God's people didn't always give Him the glory He was due. In fact, on one occasion Solomon took credit for the glory that was rightfully God's. Second Chronicles relates the story of the state visit of the Queen of Sheba to King Solomon's court. When she had tested his wisdom, surveyed all his wealth, and viewed the Temple he had built, "she was breathless" (9:4). "Behold, half of the greatness of your wisdom was not told me," she said (v. 6), and then went on to describe how wonderful and wise Solomon was, how lucky his servants were, what great things he had done, including, no doubt, what a marvelous Temple he had built. Evidently she left for home without ever realizing that it was God's glory that dwelt in the Temple, not Solomon's. Unfortunately, the record doesn't reveal that Solomon ever corrected her.

From that point on, we see a gradual but marked decline of the Temple and its glory. The *shekinah* is no longer mentioned.

Idolatry slowly moved in on God's glory, beginning during the latter part of Solomon's reign (1 Kings 11:4). Worship of the true God in His own Temple had all but disappeared by the time the prophet Ezekiel came along.

From Glory to Shame

When God's people fell into sin and failed to honor Him, God withdrew His glory. Ezekiel saw this in a vision, recorded in Ezekiel 8. In that vision, God showed Ezekiel the idol worship being carried on right inside the Temple grounds. What Ezekiel saw greatly disturbed him: "So I entered and looked, and behold, every form of creeping things and beasts and detestable things, with all the idols of the house of Israel, were carved on the wall all around" (v. 10). Then he went into the inner court of the Lord's house, and there he saw men with their backs toward the Temple of the Lord, bowed down with their faces toward the east, worshiping the sun (v. 16).

No wonder Ezekiel was so disturbed. God wasn't being worshiped and glorified in His own Temple—Satan was. God cannot tolerate sin in His presence (Habakkuk 1:13); so He vacated His own Temple. The withdrawal of God's glory occurred in progressive stages, almost as if God left reluctantly and in great sadness. Ezekiel recounts how the glory retreated step by step. The glory rose up from the sculptured cherub and stood over the doorway (Ezekiel 9:3). Next, the glory moved from the doorway and rested on the wings of the living cherubim of Ezekiel's vision (10:18). From there, it hovered over the east gate of the Temple (10:19). Then it went up from the middle of Jerusalem and stood on a mountain to the east (11:23). Finally the manifestation of glory was no longer visible, for it returned to heaven. God removed His glory from the Temple and returned it to His throne.

Now instead of glory shining in the midst of the building, it was as if the word *Ichabod*, meaning "the glory has departed" (1 Samuel 4:21), had been carved into the doorposts. Sadly, the day had come when even the magnificent Temple was no longer a fit receptacle for God's glory. No wonder God finally allowed the Babylonians to burn the building down. God's glory was gone! Would it ever come back?

Glory Incarnate

God's glory did return, many centuries later. John 1:14 tells us: "The Word became flesh, and dwelt among us, and we beheld His glory, glory as of the only begotten from the Father, full of grace and truth."

God's glory came back in the person of our Lord Jesus Christ. When was it most fully manifested? On the mountaintop at the time of the Transfiguration (Luke 9:28-36). There, for a few minutes, in the presence of three disciples, the Son of God allowed all His splendor to shine through. Here was glory—not as a glow in the Garden or as a reflection on Moses' face or in the brightness of the Tabernacle or Temple, but glory intrinsic to the God man, Jesus Christ.

Although the glory of Christ is permanent, like His other attributes, this manifestation of it was only temporary. One day wicked men arrested Him, took Him away, condemned Him falsely, hideously tortured Him, and nailed Him to a cross, and He died. They wanted to dispose of the greatest expression ever of God's glory.

But they could not extinguish that glory. Our Lord rose again from the dead. Even the terrible wounds in His body were glorified. His earthly work was ended; He ascended to heaven.

Glory to Come

Will God's glory ever be manifested again? Our Lord gave the answer in Matthew 24, His great discourse on the Mount of Olives. Jesus told the disciples of a time of great tribulation that's coming. He outlined for them the events surrounding His return to this world. When Jesus descends bodily from heaven, something spectacular will happen: "And then the sign of the Son of Man will appear in the sky, and then all the tribes of the earth will mourn, and they will see the Son of Man coming on the clouds of the sky with power and great glory" (v. 30).

What is the sign Jesus speaks of? It is the visible manifestation of His glory. It is the total brilliance of God coming down out of heaven in the person of our Lord. It is the *shekinah* glory revealed in His body, just as it was briefly displayed to three disciples on the Mount of Transfiguration.

Once again sinful men will try to extinguish it. They will oppose Him, even though He comes as "King of kings, and Lord of lords" (Revelation 19:16). When they see His flaming glory descending out of the sky, they will fire off their missiles, hoping to blow that glory out of the sky.

But they won't be able to do it. With only a word, Jesus will exterminate those who seek to restrain His glory. From that time on, He will rule the nations with a rod of iron and will reign on David's throne with power and glory—far greater glory than He revealed at His first advent.

Do you want to know something exciting? We who know Him are going to be there! All the dead in Christ, as well as those caught up with Him at the Rapture, will return with Him in His glory. Paul told the Colossian church, "When Christ, who is our life, is revealed, then you also will be revealed with Him in glory" (Colossians 3:4). The promise extends to all who have trusted Him. When He comes back, He will give us new, glorified bodies fit to enjoy His glorious presence forever.

Have you ever wondered what we will do for all eternity? In the book of Revelation we learn the answer:

> *After these things I looked, and behold, a great multitude which no one could count, from every nation and all tribes and peoples and tongues, standing before the throne and before the Lamb, clothed in white robes, and palm branches were in their hands; and they cry out with a loud voice, saying, "Salvation to our God who sits on the throne, and to the Lamb."*
>
> —REVELATION 7:9, 10

Not only will we give God glory, we also will see His glory for all eternity. Revelation 21 describes "the holy city, Jerusalem, coming down out of heaven from God, having the glory of God. . . . And the city has no need of the sun or of the moon to shine on it, for the glory of God has illumined it, and its lamp is the Lamb" (vv. 10, 11, 23).

Glory in the Present

That's a brief look at the glory of God in the past and a glimpse of the glory that shall be, as revealed in Scripture. But where is the glory of God right now?

In this age, God's glory is manifest in His people, the church. It is our privilege, our purpose, and our duty to manifest the glory of God. Paul tells us that we are a holy temple housing the glory of God (Ephesians 2:21, 22). The purpose God has left us on this earth for is "to give the Light of the knowledge of the glory of God in the face of Christ" (2 Corinthians 4:6).

Although we are earthen vessels—clay pots, if you will—we carry within us the glory of God (2 Corinthians 4:7). God has chosen the humble things of this world to bring glory to Himself (1 Corinthians 1:26-31). He transforms us by the power of the Holy Spirit and allows us to radiate that glory. If the world is ever going to get the message of that glory, it must come through us. People must see "Christ in [us], the hope of glory" (Colossians 1:27). The more mature we are, the more we can be used to radiate God's glory. "Whether, then, you eat or drink or whatever you do, do all to the glory of God" (1 Corinthians 10:31).

GLORY FOR HIS NAME

Some Christians witness for the Lord out of a sense of obedience, because they are commanded to do so. Others share the Gospel because of their love and concern for the lost. Those are worthy motives, but not the highest one.

The supreme motive for evangelism should be the glory of God. That is what moved the apostle Paul. He labored, evangelized, preached, and poured out his heart "for His name's sake" (Romans 1:5). Paul loved the lost and was obedient to Christ's command to evangelize. But the passionate desire of Paul's heart was to bring others to the Savior so He might get the glory due Him. If God is God and God alone and the sole Creator and the Lord of men, He has a right to exclusive worship and a right to be jealous if He is not worshiped.

Henry Martyn, that godly missionary to India, watched people bowing down before their idols. Seeing those people prostrate before Hindu gods "excited more horror in me than I can well express. . . . I could not endure existence if Jesus was not glorified. It would be hell to me."

I must confess that God has rebuked me time and again because I don't always feel that way. It hasn't always been "hell to me" to see someone who does not glorify Jesus Christ. But I pray continually that God will give me such a love for the glory of Jesus that it will break my heart every time someone doesn't give my Lord the glory He deserves.

He is most worthy of glory.

For this reason also God highly exalted Him, and bestowed on Him the name which is above every name, so that at the name of Jesus every knee will bow, of those who are in heaven and on earth and under the earth, and that every tongue will confess that Jesus Christ is Lord, to the glory of God the Father.

—PHILIPPIANS 2:9-11

The hymn writer pleads eloquently:

Let ev'ry kindred, ev'ry tribe,
On this terrestrial ball,
To Him all majesty ascribe,
And crown Him Lord of all.

The glory of God—we see it in the heavens, in the earth, in salvation, in Christian living, in the promised return of Christ, in every dimension of life. I call it the Master Purpose for unlocking all the spiritual riches hidden in Jesus Christ. Now if that is the Master Purpose of living, how can we build upon it? How, practically, can we glorify God? For that we need another key—the Master Plan.

3

THE
MASTER PLAN

How to Glorify God

A Cincinnati newspaper printed an item about a local woman who pulled up at a stoplight and noticed the car in front of her was sporting a HONK IF YOU LOVE JESUS bumper sticker. The woman gave a friendly toot on her horn and was shocked when the driver in front of her turned angrily and flashed an obscene gesture.

Lesson number one in how to be a good testimony: Don't do that!

Too many in the church today seem prone to reduce their faith to bumper-sticker expressions, as if aphorisms and symbolism could somehow convey to the world the majesty and glory of our God. Of course they can't. Glorifying God is more than pasting an adage on your car, even if you drive with good manners.

How does a person glorify God? That is not a theoretical or trivial question. In fact, no question is more practical or more significant. The supreme purpose in life for any man or woman—for anyone who has ever been born into this world—is to glorify God. That is what living is all about. Glorifying God is the end result of the Christian life. Spiritual maturity is simply concentrating and focusing on the person of God until we are caught up in His majesty and His glory.

WHY GLORIFY GOD?

Let's look briefly at the *why* before we get to the *how*. The most obvious reason to glorify God is that He created us. Psalm 100:3

states it simply: "It is He who has made us." Compare that with Romans 11:36: "For from Him and through Him and to Him are all things. To Him be the glory forever. Amen." Why does God deserve glory? Because He gave us our being, our life, and everything we have and are. That is reason number one.

Second, we ought to glorify God because He made everything to give Him glory. Creation shows His attributes, His power, His love, His mercy, His wisdom, and His grace. All creation gives Him glory. The stars do: "The heavens are telling of the glory of God" (Psalm 19:1). Animals do: "The beasts of the field will glorify Me" (Isaiah 43:20). The angels do. At the birth of Christ they said, "Glory to God in the highest" (Luke 2:14).

Animals, which are lower than man in the rank of creation, glorify God. Angels, who are higher in rank than man (Hebrews 2:7), glorify Him too. Can we do less than give Him the glory due His name?

God even gets glory out of unbelievers who do not choose to glorify Him. Chalk this up as reason number three: God judges those who refuse to glorify Him. A good example is the pharaoh who was on the throne at the time God miraculously released Israel from the Egyptians' cruel bondage. This man fought against God to the bitter end. But God declared, "I will be honored through Pharaoh" (Exodus 14:17). And He was; His power was demonstrated even in Pharaoh's death. Sooner or later everyone will give God glory—willingly or unwillingly.

HOW TO GLORIFY GOD

I would like to suggest thirteen practical ways—not in any particular order of importance—to glorify God.

Receive the Lord Jesus Christ as Your Savior

Trust Christ. That's basic. You cannot even begin to give God glory until you come to Christ. Up to that point, you haven't acknowledged God. To come to Christ is to give Him glory. "For this reason also, God highly exalted Him, and bestowed on Him the name which is above every name, so that at the name of Jesus every knee will bow, of those who are in heaven and on earth and under the earth, and that every tongue will confess that Jesus Christ is Lord, to the glory of God the Father" (Philippians 2:9-11). God is glorified when we bow and confess Jesus as Lord. If you want to give God glory, begin here.

Make it the Aim of Your Life to Glorify God

God's glory must be our primary goal in everything. You will never glorify God in your life until you aim at it. The command in 1 Corinthians 10:31 is all-inclusive: "Whether, then, you eat or drink or whatever you do, do all to the glory of God." We are commanded to glorify Him even when we eat and drink! How much more should we seek to glorify Him in the important things of life? That is what is meant by aiming at His glory. Our Lord said, "I do not seek My glory" (John 8:50). In other words: "I live to bring God glory. I live to radiate His attributes. I live to adorn the doctrine of God. I live to exalt God in the eyes of the world. This is the purpose of My life."

The first principle of aiming for the glory of God is to *be willing to sacrifice self and self-glory.* Hypocrites come along and try to steal the glory of God. They want a little glory for themselves. Remember the almsgivers whom Jesus warned about in Matthew 6:1-4? "When you give to the poor," Jesus said, "do not sound a trumpet before you, as the hypocrites do in the synagogues and in the streets, so that they may be honored by men" (v. 2). Can you imagine that? Such fellows brought along a trumpeter to play a little fanfare as they arrived at the Temple to drop their coins in the box. "Here I am, folks. See me?" Plunk, plunk. Note that the Lord said they did it so men would honor them. God does not reward the kind of giving that competes for His glory.

Even sincere Christians have to beware of trying to steal glory from God. A young man once came up to D. L. Moody and said, "Mr. Moody, we've just been to an all-night prayer meeting. See how our faces shine!" Moody quietly replied, "Moses knew not that his face shone" (see Exodus 34:29). Don't try to take any glory from God. You can't get it anyway, and you'll lose God's blessing as well.

Another way to aim your life to the glory of God is to *prefer Him above all else*. Place Him above all things—money, fame, honor, success, friends, even family. I can think of times when I have gone to speak somewhere, and in the back of my mind I found myself thinking, *I hope they like me. My, I'll bet they'll really like me*. That is disgusting. If what I say is not for the glory of God, but for myself, I might as well shut my mouth. If I teach a Bible study for my own glory, God's blessing is not on it. We must prefer His glory above everything else.

You'll probably have to pay a high price in order to maintain the right perspective. It might even cost you some friends. In Exodus 32 some people paid just such a price. In an orgy of idolatry at the foot of the mountain, the Israelites built a golden calf and began to worship it in a wild, raucous manner. This occurred *while* Moses was receiving the Ten Commandments, just after the people had promised to obey God alone! When Moses came down and saw it, he was angry. He said, "Whoever is for the LORD, come to me!" (v. 26). All the sons of Levi, the priests, came forward. Then Moses said, "Thus says the LORD, the God of Israel, 'Every man of you put his sword upon his thigh, and go back and forth from gate to gate in the camp, and kill every man his brother, and every man his friend, and every man his neighbor'" (v. 27). Would they carry out that order? They did, and 3,000 fell (v. 28). You see, the glory of God was at stake. And God shares His glory with no other. Those people had to pay the price of actually killing those they loved—for the sake of the glory of God.

Another crucial way of aiming at God's glory is to *be content to do His will at any cost*. Jesus prayed, "Now My soul has become troubled; and what shall I say, 'Father, save Me from this hour'? But for this purpose I came to this hour. Father, glorify Your name" (John 12:27, 28). And in the Garden of Gethsemane Jesus prayed, "Father, if You are willing, remove this cup from Me; yet not My will, but Yours be done" (Luke 22:42). In other words, "Father, if You are going to get glory out of this, I submit to it. Glorify Your name, Father, whatever it costs Me."

Aiming at God's glory also means that *we suffer when He suffers*—we hurt when God is dishonored. Remember Psalm 69:9: "For zeal for Your house has consumed me, and the reproaches of those who reproach You have fallen on me." David was saying, "I hurt when God's name is reproached."

I remember receiving a letter from a seventeen-year-old girl whom my sister had the privilege of leading to Christ. The problems in her background were just unbelievable. After receiving Christ, she had to return to her home in a distant city, with no Christian friends, no spiritual instruction, with nothing except her Bible and people praying for her. Several months later she wrote:

> I hope everything is well with you. I have really begun to put things together in the Bible. By reading the Old Testament I have been able to see that God deserves much more recognition than He's getting. I can see how He gave people so many chances and how they continued to break His heart by worshiping idols and sinning. God wanted the Israelites to sacrifice lambs, goats, oxen and things like that as an atonement to Him for sin. He is God, after all, and He had to have some payment for the trouble and the sins of men.
>
> To think that God actually talked and was in the visible presence of these people and yet they kept on complaining and sinning! I can almost feel the unbearable sadness that God feels when someone rejects and doesn't glorify Him. He's God! He made us. He gave us everything. We continue to doubt and reject Him. It's awful! When I think of how I hurt Him, I hope I can someday make it up.
>
> I have a soft spot in my heart for God. I can feel His jealousy now when I see people worshiping idols and other gods. It's all so clear to me that God must be glorified. He deserves it, and it's long overdue.
>
> I can't wait to just tell Jesus, and thus God indirectly, that I love Him and just kiss the ground He walks on because He should be worshiped. I want God to be God and to take His rightful place. I'm tired of the way people put Him down.

All by herself, with her Bible and the Holy Spirit, that young girl came to realize that the glory of God was what life was all about. I know some people who have been Christians for decades and haven't learned this truth. The purpose of our existence is to give God glory, and part of that means hurting when He is reproached.

If you would aim at God's glory, you must also *be content to go unrecognized as long as God gets the glory*. The life of Paul gives us an excellent illustration. His great goal was to exalt God through Jesus Christ. He did that actively until the time came when he was shut up in prison. Had that happened to us, we might have considered ourselves shelved. But Paul took it in stride, because he was trusting God that even this would be a means of glorifying Him. And it was. Paul was used of the Lord while in prison to write several of the books of the New Testament. His ministry during those difficult days still reaps a harvest nearly two millennia later!

But while Paul was being held, some on the outside were seeking to hurt him. He described them as those who "proclaim Christ out of selfish ambition rather than from pure motives, thinking to cause me distress in my imprisonment" (Philippians 1:17). That could have been painful for Paul. While he was confined in that rotten prison, others were free on the outside—free to preach, free to teach, and free to win the love of those brought to Christ.

How did Paul react? "What then? Only that in every way, whether in pretense or in truth, Christ is proclaimed; and in this I rejoice. Yes, and I will rejoice" (v. 18). The apostle didn't care who got the credit, as long as the Lord was glorified.

How about you? What are your inner feelings when someone gains honor at your expense? How do you react? One mark of spiritual maturity is being willing to let others have the credit. How you respond will reveal whether you are concerned with His glory or with your own.

Confess Your Sins

Perhaps you hadn't thought of it, but when you confess your own sin, you glorify God.

A good illustration comes from the story of Achan (Joshua 7).

You remember how, in direct violation of God's orders, this man gathered up part of the spoils after the fall of Jericho. *No one will know; no one will find out,* he thought as he buried them in a hole under his tent. Perhaps he even thought, *God will never know. He can't see through the dirt.* But God did know, and Achan was exposed. What did Joshua say? "My son, I implore you, give glory to the LORD, the God of Israel . . . and tell me now what you have done" (v. 19).

Confession of sin glorifies God because if you excuse your sin, you impugn God. In effect, you absolve yourself of responsibility and blame God for letting you get into a mess. Adam illustrates this. When God confronted him, what was his excuse? "The woman whom You gave to be with me, she gave me from the tree, and I ate" (Genesis 3:12). He was practically saying, "You did it, God. If You hadn't given me this woman, none of this would ever have happened."

To do that is to blame God and thus to assign guilt to Him. But God is never at fault when we sin. Implying that He is somehow responsible maligns His holiness. So those who try to sneak out from under the absolute responsibility for their own sin commit a grievous sin against the glory of God.

A helpful illustration comes from 1 Samuel. The Israelites had not paid any attention to God for years until they got into a big battle with the Philistines. Someone said, "We're in trouble! We have to get God up here. Go down and get the ark." The ark represented God's presence. It was supposed to stay in the most holy place in the Tabernacle. But the backslidden nation thought they could put it to use in battle like a super-good-luck charm.

When the ark arrived on the front line, the people were delirious: "As the ark of the covenant of the LORD came into the camp, all Israel shouted with a great shout, so that the earth resounded" (1 Samuel 4:5).

But the ploy didn't work. The Philistines captured the ark and stuck it in the temple of Dagon, their false god. They were about to discover that God was not to be trifled with! God began chopping away at the idol Dagon (5:1-4). In the morning the Philistines found

Dagon on his face before the ark. They set him back up, but the next day he was prostrate again, with his head and hands broken off. Only his stone trunk was intact. And God was not through. "Now the hand of the LORD was heavy on the Ashdodites, and He ravaged them and smote them with tumors" (5:6). God was smiting them for their mistreatment of the ark.

Their response was most interesting. They cried out to heaven (v. 12). Chapter 6 relates that they decided to return the ark and to appease God by making a trespass offering. Apparently a plague of mice had struck the Philistines at the same time. So, following their pagan custom, they made a votive offering, which included likenesses of the diseased parts. They made golden images of the tumors and mice in order to "give glory to the God of Israel" (v. 5).

That act gave glory to God because it constituted a confession of sin. It was an acknowledgment that the evil that had befallen them resulted from their offending God. Once they came and made their offerings and confession, they exonerated God and exalted His holy response to their evil. They said in effect, "God, You had a right to act as You did, because of what we did." That gave God glory.

When chastisement or discipline from God comes into your life, react by saying, "God, I deserve every bit of it! I know that because You are holy, You had to do what You did." That gives God glory.

First John 1:9 says, "If we confess our sins, He is faithful and righteous to forgive us our sins and to cleanse us from all unrighteousness." We will discuss confession of sin in more detail in chapter 6, but let me point out that the Greek word for "confess" is *homologeo*, meaning "to say the same thing." To confess means to agree with God that sin is all our fault and to repent. That act glorifies God. We don't have to beg God for forgiveness. He is faithful and just to forgive as soon as we agree with Him.

Trust God

Romans 4:20 says that Abraham was "strong in faith, giving glory to God." God is glorified when we trust Him. Unbelief doubts God and implies that He is not to be trusted. That detracts from His glory.

Sometimes I think that the greatest problem in letting the world know about God's glory is that the message has to go through us! We like to quote the verse, "My God will supply all your needs according to His riches in glory in Christ Jesus" (Philippians 4:19). But then some crisis comes into our lives, and we collapse. Sometimes everyone at the job and at home knows it. Then people say, "Some kind of God you have! You don't even trust Him yourself." God is glorified when we believe in Him, when we rest in His full assurance. That gives Him glory.

Daniel's three friends are a classic example of those who trusted God in the face of a severe trial. When about to be thrown into the fiery furnace, they didn't say, "We have a practical problem. What verse applies here?" They simply made a flat announcement: "Our God whom we serve is able to deliver us from the furnace of blazing fire; and He will deliver us out of your hand, O king" (Daniel 3:17). Then they said, "*But even if he does not*, let it be known to you, O king, that we are not going to serve your gods or worship the golden image that you have set up" (v. 18, emphasis added). If they had panicked, fallen to the ground, and groveled in the dirt before the golden image, that would not have glorified God. But because they trusted Him with their lives, He was glorified before an entire nation!

God is always glorified when we trust Him. Do you think God keeps His word? Of course He does. But do you live as if He keeps His word? That's a more difficult question to answer yes to. That's why the world often isn't too sure what kind of God we have. Let's glorify God by trusting Him. Not to trust Him is the same as calling Him a liar (1 John 5:10).

Bear Fruit

God is glorified when we bear abundant fruit. In John 15:8 Jesus told the disciples, "My Father is glorified by this, that you bear much fruit." Why? Because then the world can see the results of a Spirit-filled life.

The Bible echoes this thought repeatedly: ". . . having been filled with the fruit of righteousness which comes through Jesus Christ, to the glory and praise of God" (Philippians 1:11). God planted the seed, and He expects fruit. His character is at stake in the eyes of men who will take note of fruitfulness in the life of the Christian. "But you are a chosen race, a royal priesthood, a holy nation, a people for God's own possession, so that you may proclaim the excellencies of Him who has called you out of darkness into His marvelous light" (1 Peter 2:9). That is what we are here for—to put God on display to the world.

Colossians 1:10 takes us a step further: "so that you will walk in a manner worthy of the Lord, to please Him in all respects, bearing fruit in every good work." Good works are fruit. When we live a life of good works, the world will see and glorify our Father in heaven.

Give Praise to God

Psalm 50:23 says, "He who offers a sacrifice of thanksgiving honors Me." Praise honors God. One way to offer praise is to recite God's wonderful works. New Christians will sometimes ask me if there is any reason to study the Old Testament. I always give an emphatic yes. God wrote it, and anything that God wrote, I want to read. When I was courting my wife, she used to write me little notes. I loved them and read them over again and again. When you love someone, you are interested in what that special person has to say. The same is true of the Old Testament. I love God; therefore I want to read what He wrote.

One reason we should study the Old Testament is to know what God has done in history so we can recite it to others. We can say, "God did this and this and this—how wonderful are His works!" The record of the past is a continual reminder that He has never proved unfaithful in history. What did the disciples speak of on the day of Pentecost, in languages they had never learned? "The mighty deeds of God" (Acts 2:11). Because the Jews traditionally exalted God for His wondrous works, this outburst of praise caught their attention.

Another way to praise God is to give Him credit for everything. Remember how Joab fought against Rabbah and won the victory? When he got possession of the enemy's crown, he sent for David so he could present the crown to him (2 Samuel 12:26-31). I've often thought that is a good illustration of how the Christian acts toward the Master—or should. You win a victory in your life, but you don't wear the crown. You give it to the Lord, who has won the victory for you.

Endure Suffering

The Bible is full of examples of those who suffered for the cause of God. Jeremiah was imprisoned, and according to tradition Isaiah was sawn in two. Stephen was stoned to death. Church history records that all the apostles (except John), including Paul, met with violent deaths. But like those mentioned in Revelation 12:11, "they did not love their life even when faced with death."

Our Lord told Peter that he would die by crucifixion in order to glorify God (John 21:18, 19). Peter himself underscored that concept when he wrote, "If you are reviled for the name of Christ, you are blessed, because the Spirit of glory and of God rests on you . . . but if anyone suffers as a Christian, he is not to be ashamed, but is to glorify God" (1 Peter 4:14, 16). When you suffer for Christ's sake, when you stand in front of the world and speak the truth and take the abuse, when you confront the system with the claims of Jesus Christ in boldness and courage, you glorify God. What a tremendous thing it is to be called to suffer for His sake!

Be Content

Discontent characterizes the age in which we live. We may be discontent about ourselves and about our circumstances. But who made us? God. And He promises to supply all our needs. When we are content, we acknowledge God's sovereignty in our lives, and that gives Him glory. If we are discontent, it's the same as questioning God's wisdom. That doesn't glorify Him.

Paul testified, "I have learned to be content in whatever circumstances I am. I know how to get along with humble means, and I also know how to live in prosperity; in any and every circumstance I have learned the secret of being filled and going hungry, both of having abundance and suffering need" (Philippians 4:11, 12).

This is the same man who cataloged his suffering in 2 Corinthians 11—his beatings, his imprisonments, his stonings, his shipwrecks, his perils, his weariness and pain, his hunger and thirst, his cold and nakedness.

How do you think Paul could give God glory in all that? He understood God's working in his life, and he was confident that God would use all things—poverty as well as abundance, comfort as well as pain—for Paul's good and God's glory (Romans 8:28). He said, "I will not boast, except in regard to my weaknesses" (2 Corinthians 12:5). He didn't say, "I'll give God glory in spite of my pain." He said, "I will give God glory because of it." Now that's a contented man. But his perspective should be the attitude of every Christian.

Let me emphasize once again: Discontent is a sin because it robs God of glory. A Christian who is discontented for any reason— home, job, financial status, location, husband or wife or kids—is a terrible testimony about the goodness of our God. What kind of God do we have? Is He really sovereign? Can He really be trusted? Can we be content in whatever circumstances He places us? David said, "The LORD is the portion of my inheritance. . . . The lines have fallen to me in pleasant places" (Psalm 16:5, 6). David was saying, "Since the Lord is the portion of my inheritance, since it is the Lord whom I have received, the boundaries He gives me in life are pleasant." He went on to say, "Indeed, my heritage is beautiful to me. I will bless the LORD" (vv. 6, 7).

Glorifying God means that we praise Him with a full heart in absolute contentment, knowing that our lot is God's plan for us now. Accepting it with contentment gives Him glory.

Pray According to God's Will

Jesus said, "Whatever you ask in My name, that will I do, that the Father may be glorified in the Son" (John 14:13). What a promise! If I were not a Christian, and someone told me that verse, that might be enough to convince me to become a believer—just to know there is a God available to supply everything I ask for.

But there is one qualification: "whatever you ask in My name." Praying in Jesus' name does not mean sticking a cursory "in Jesus' name, amen" onto the end of our prayers to get what we want. Our Lord wasn't giving His disciples some kind of holy abracadabra. Jesus' name signifies all that He is and all that He would want. Praying in His name means praying in accordance with His character and His will. As I get to know Christ better and understand His will, I ask what I do because I feel it is what Jesus would want. That's what praying in Jesus' name means. It is not possible to invoke Jesus' name for anything that is contrary to His character.

Jesus promised that if we ask in His name, He will do what we ask, "so that the Father may be glorified in the Son." Why does God, who already knows our hearts, want us to pray? So He can glorify Himself in the answer. Have you ever heard someone stand up in a testimony meeting and say, "Such and such a thing was taking place, and we prayed about it, and God answered our prayer"? And everyone says, "Praise the Lord!" That's the point. When you pray, and God displays His power, He gets the glory. "Father, there's a sick person here. Heal him, that Your glory may be known." That's how to pray. Not merely, "Heal that person because we don't want to lose him."

God delights to reveal His glory in answered prayer. That is why He commands us to pray—so He can show us His greatness and we can give Him the praise He's worthy to receive. People who never pray miss one of the most effective ways to glorify God.

Proclaim God's Word

God gave us His Word because He wants to communicate with us. When we take His Word and communicate it to others, we share with them the mind of God. Consequently He is glorified because He is able to speak. Thus when we declare God's Word, we are glorifying Him.

Paul wrote, "Brethren, pray for us that the word of the Lord will spread rapidly and be glorified, just as it did also with you" (2 Thessalonians 3:1). How was the Word glorified through those believers? Because they heard it and believed. They trusted Christ and were born again—and God got the glory.

If I enter the pulpit only to give my opinions, God would not get the glory. People might go out saying, "Isn't John MacArthur clever?" Well, let me tell you, I know from personal acquaintance that he isn't! He has to spend hours each day just trying to figure out what God is saying, let alone add any of his own clever thoughts. But if the Word is proclaimed, people leave saying, "Isn't God wonderful!" When they hear God speaking in His Word and respond, that brings glory to Him.

Paul preached on a certain Sabbath at Antioch, and Scripture tells us, "When the Gentiles heard this, they began rejoicing and glorifying the word of the Lord" (Acts 13:48). They heard Paul preach the Word, and they glorified God.

Presenting the Word clearly and accurately always gives Him glory. Every time a Sunday school teacher teaches a class of kids, every time a Bible study leader opens the Word in someone's living room, every time a father sits down with his family and starts talking about the Word of God, God is glorified. We honor Him by making His Word known and understood.

Lead Others to Christ

God also gets glory when people are redeemed. He is glorified when Satan's prison is broken open and men and women are turned loose from the power of the evil one. God wants a great number of people giving Him glory. So the more people who get converted, the more thanksgiving is going on; and the more thanksgiving is going on, the more there are in the choir singing "Hallelujah!" That's the idea. (See 2 Corinthians 4:15.)

God's glory shines from many angles in the salvation of souls. For one thing, when someone is transformed by the power of Christ, that individual gives Him glory. For another thing, when someone passes from death unto life, the rest of us who already know the Lord give Him glory. When a woman comes along and says, "Say, I must tell you, my husband for whom we've been in prayer came to know Christ this week!" we say, "Praise the Lord!" We give glory to God. So not only has another individual been added to the choir of the "Hallelujah Chorus," but many other believers praise God as well.

God is going to display His people in heaven to the angels as a token of His wisdom forever (Ephesians 3:10). We're going to be God's trophies in heaven. All through eternity God will point to us as proof of His manifold wisdom. And the angels are going to say, "Yes! Anyone who could bring that bunch to such heights—yes, Lord, that's great wisdom!"

Listen to Ephesians 1:12: "that we who were the first to hope in Christ would be to the praise of His glory." Why does God give us an inheritance? For "the praise of His glory." Why does He give us the Holy Spirit, who is the guarantor of our inheritance until the redemption is finally carried out? "To the praise of His glory" (vv. 12, 14). You are saved from your sins in order to give God glory. That, as we have seen repeatedly, is the purpose of our existence. That is the reason we are Christians. And if we really want to give Him glory, we will have a passion to bring others to Jesus Christ.

Avoid Sexual Sin

In 1 Corinthians 6:18 Paul says, "Flee immorality." He gives three reasons why a Christian's liberty was never meant to allow sexual sin. Sexual sin harms, enslaves, and perverts (vv. 12-20).

When a Christian sins sexually, God is dishonored, because our bodies are for the Lord, one with Christ, and sanctuaries of the Holy Spirit. Sexual sin joins the Lord to a prostitute, Paul exclaims. God is thus dishonored, and the Temple desecrated. So it is unthinkable to use Christ's body for sexual sin.

A friend of mine said that he once saw a unique shrine in a Catholic church. It had a sign over it saying, THIS SHRINE IS OUT OF ORDER. DO NOT WORSHIP HERE. A similar sign would have to be hung on an immoral Christian.

Paul closes the section by saying, "Glorify God in your body" (v. 20). We are to run from the trap of illicit sex, just as Joseph ran from the arms of Potiphar's wife when she tried to seduce him (Genesis 39). God will be glorified through our purity as clean sanctuaries.

Seek Unity

If I were to pinpoint one single tragedy that has marred the testimony of the church in the world, it would be the division, conflict, discord, dissension, and disunity among us. No wonder the world has no clear understanding of the validity of Christianity when some of the biggest battles going on in the world are between Christians. The Bible says we are to love one another, so the world may know we belong to Jesus Christ. Scripture commands us, for example, not even to take a fellow Christian to court before a non-Christian. Why? So that the world might see unity of mind and purpose in the church.

Let me amplify this. Romans 15:5 says, "Now may the God who gives perseverance and encouragement grant you to be of the same mind with one another according to Christ Jesus." Our example is always Christ. How did He treat others? He treated everyone the same. God expects that of us: "so that with one accord you may with one voice glorify the God and Father of our Lord Jesus Christ" (v. 6). Paul admonished the Corinthians, "Now I exhort you, brethren, by the name of our Lord Jesus Christ, that you all agree and there be no divisions among you, but you be made complete in the same mind and in the same judgment" (1 Corinthians 1:10).

There is certainly room for different views on minor matters. We may disagree on educational issues, on economic matters, or on politics. We may have different perspectives on peripheral doctrinal questions. But we must never let our disagreements breach the fellowship and unity we have as members of the body of Christ.

On the other hand, we must never compromise essential gospel truth for the sake of external unity. We cannot stand with those who call themselves Christians but deny the essential truths of Christ's deity, salvation by grace through faith, and the inspiration and authority of Scripture. Believers who compromise on those issues in a misguided attempt to make a show of unity actually confuse unbelievers about the basic truths of Scripture. God is not glorified in that kind of compromise. We who know the Lord must stand firmly together to protect these crucial truths. We glorify God only when with one mind and one mouth we declare the message of Christ clearly and accurately to an unsaved world.

People will take notice of Christians' unity. God is not "a God of confusion" (1 Corinthians 14:33). When an unbeliever sees confusion, he assumes God must not be at work there. So God wants unity. Instead of shutting fellow believers out of our little group because they don't do all the things we do, we receive them because Christ has received them. We do this "to the glory of God" (Romans 15:7). God is glorified when there is unity among the brethren.

HOW TO ENJOY GOD

We've seen several ways to glorify God. That is only the first part of the catechism's statement: "The chief end of man is to glorify God." Now let's turn briefly to the last part of that famous statement: ". . . and to enjoy Him forever." When we live to glorify God, He responds by giving us overwhelming joy. I sometimes think that if I were any happier and had more joy, I would not be able to stand it. Life becomes thrilling in response to glorifying God.

"Well," you say, "I have a tough life. I just don't have any joy." May I suggest an answer? Start glorifying God. Like the prophet Habakkuk, your circumstances may not change, but you will. He declared, "I will rejoice in the God of my salvation" (Habakkuk 3:18). It took him an entire chapter to recite everything he knew about God, but then he came out rejoicing. That is the pattern. Live to the glory of God, and joy will come.

Joy does not necessarily always make sorrow, discouragement, pain, and failure go away, but Christians can experience supernatural joy even in the midst of those things. In fact, sin is ultimately the only thing that can steal Christians' joy. When our joy begins to fade, it is a sure sign of encroaching sin or unbelief. What can we do in times like that? Get down on our knees and confess the sin in our lives. We need to pray with David, "Restore to me the joy of Your salvation" (Psalm 51:12). Then we yield to the Holy Spirit, and joy returns.

When you see a brother without joy, you know he is failing

in the Christian life. God never expects believers to be downcast, depressed, or discouraged. He wants us to be joyous even in the midst of great trouble. Jesus said, "These things I have spoken to you so that My joy may be in you, and that your joy may be made full" (John 15:11). Paul, Peter, James, and the other apostles all found full joy even in the midst of great persecution and distress. That joy is the birthright of every believer, and those who do not seize it are missing a very important—and very practical—truth.

Did you realize that being filled with the Spirit and having joy is virtually the same thing? One of the fruits of the Spirit is "joy" (Galatians 5:22, 23). Joy is the inevitable by-product of living a Spirit-controlled life. Acts 13:52 tells us that "the disciples were continually filled with joy and with the Holy Spirit." The two go together. "For the kingdom of God is not eating and drinking, but righteousness and peace and joy in the Holy Spirit" (Romans 14:17). The Spirit-filled life brings its own built-in joy.

ENJOYING GOD FOREVER

The catechism says that we will enjoy God forever. We can know God and enjoy Him now. We can have joy in God now and in the future. Listen to the marvelous words of Psalm 73:25, 26: "Whom have I in heaven but You? And besides You, I desire nothing on earth. My flesh and my heart may fail, but God is the strength of my heart and my portion forever." The psalmist was excited about enjoying God both now and for all eternity. Our joy in heaven will be the same joy we experience here, but heaven will be the full expression of that joy, totally unencumbered by sin.

Jesus desires that His joy remain in us (John 15:11). His joy that we know in part now is what we will know perfectly in heaven. Perhaps the greatest promise in all the Bible is 1 Thessalonians 4:17: "We shall always be with the Lord." Now that's joy!

"The chief end of man is to glorify God and to enjoy Him forever!" That's a very old key to spiritual growth, but one that unlocks a crucial door.

4

OBEDIENCE

Unlocking the Servants' Quarters

Ferdinand Waldo Demara, Jr., otherwise known as the Great Impostor, was a high-school dropout. A book and movie chronicled the story of his life and the many occupations he pursued. Without any credentials or qualifications, he served at various times as a university executive, a psychology professor, a Trappist monk, assistant warden of a Texas prison, and a Canadian navy surgeon in Korea. In his role as surgeon, Demara did tonsillectomies, amputated limbs, and even removed a bullet from a man's chest. Yet the only medical knowledge he had was what he gleaned from books onboard his ship! For a while, this man was a teacher in my high school. In fact, many felt he was the best teacher there!

How did Ferdinand Demara find employment in so many unlikely roles? He would falsify evidence, forge identity papers, and brazenly feign, simulate, or fake his way through whatever functions were necessary to confirm his claim to be something he wasn't.

I think of Demara often as a symbol of the way many professing Christians live. Did you realize that the church is loaded with impostors? Scripture repeatedly makes this clear. Paul warned Timothy, "Evil men and impostors will proceed from bad to worse, deceiving and being deceived" (2 Timothy 3:13). When Paul left Ephesus, he told the elders of the church there, "I know that after my departure savage wolves will come in among you, not sparing the flock" (Acts 20:29). Jesus gave His disciples a similar warning: "Beware of the false prophets, who come to you in sheep's clothing, but inwardly are ravenous wolves" (Matthew 7:15). Our Lord's parable of the wheat and the tares (Matthew 13:24-30, 36-43) is a reminder that Satan specializes in planting phony believers among the true.

We dare not forget those warnings. Too many people in today's church are eager to embrace and include everyone who claims to be a Christian. Not wanting to be divisive, they fear challenging anyone's profession of faith. As a consequence, many churches today are filled with people who claim Jesus as Savior but whose behavior denies that He is Lord. The apostles recorded numerous warnings for the early church about evil influences that were creeping into the church through bogus Christians and false teachers. We must be equally circumspect, on guard against the same diabolical influences in the contemporary church.

That brings up an interesting and vital question: How can you tell genuine Christians from the impostors? There are a number of criteria, but among the most important is the matter of obedience. A person may profess faith in Christ, yet live a life of disobedience to the One he professes as Lord. Something is terribly wrong there. Our Savior asked the sobering question, "Why do you call Me, 'Lord, Lord,' and do not do what I say?" (Luke 6:46).

People have a right to be suspicious of one who says he believes in Jesus but fails to live up to that claim. James declared that genuine faith must result in a life of good works (James 2:14-26). If you really believe in God and in His Son, there should be evidence of it in the way you live, in the things you say, and in the things you do. There is an inseparable relationship between obedience and faith—like two sides of a coin. It is impossible to detach one from the other, though many today are trying very hard to devise a doctrine of "faith" that is disjointed from obedience.[1]

NOAH: A LIFE OF OBEDIENT FAITH

We might turn to a number of people in the Bible to illustrate a faith that obeys, but I can think of no greater example than Noah. Noah took one further step than the two most important earlier examples of faith, Abel and Enoch. Abel illustrates godly *worship*. Enoch embodies a godly *walk*. Noah depicts godly *work*. In fact, Noah worshiped, walked, and worked. You have to worship God if you are going to walk with Him, and you have to walk with Him before you can work for Him. That is God's pattern.

Noah's faith and obedience went far beyond human reason. What he did does not even make sense to the average mind. Unless a man knows God personally and has some kind of supernatural spiritual insight, he would be a blathering idiot to do what Noah did.

That's precisely why Noah's faith is so remarkable. He hadn't seen anything tangible or visible to establish his trust in God, but God's Word was enough for him. His life of faith and obedience may be summed up in two traits. First, he responded to God's Word. Second, he rebuked the world.

NOAH RESPONDED TO GOD'S WORD

Hebrews 11:7 tells us, "By faith Noah, being warned by God about things not yet seen, in reverence prepared an ark for the salvation of his household." He believed God—so much so that he built an ark. Now it might appear on the surface that Noah was somewhat foolhardy. It certainly appeared that way to his neighbors. They had never seen a drop of rain. How they must have laughed at his construction project! Why did he do what he did? Because God said to him, "Noah, judgment is coming. I'm going to destroy the world by water. You'd better build a boat." So Noah dropped everything and spent more than a hundred years obeying God's command.

I don't know about you, but after seventy or eighty years I'd begin to wonder. After all, Noah lived in Mesopotamia, between the Tigris and Euphrates Rivers, miles from any ocean. But faith responds to God's Word. It doesn't question—it just obeys.

Noah was a human being, just as we are. He had a lot of things to do to occupy his time. For him to give up such an immense span of his life to construct a huge boat took a serious commitment. He listened to God, and then he spent his life obeying what God said. Isn't that amazing? It would have been one thing for him to run out and secure the lumber, but it was something else to see him a hundred years later still smearing bitumen on the structure. Some of us believe God, and we run out and make a start, but that's that. We never get much past that point. Noah continued in his obedience. Jesus said perseverance is the mark of His true disciples (John 8:31). Noah was absolutely convinced of the authority that lay behind the command to him. One warning was enough for him.

Someone might argue that Noah obeyed God out of fear of the consequences. But such is not the case. Hebrews 11:7 tells us that his motivation was "reverence" for God, not abject fear. Noah obeyed because he revered God's Word. The implication is that Noah acted with pious care. He treated the message of God with great reverence and prepared the ark for saving not only himself, but also his wife, his three sons (Shem, Ham, and Japheth), and their wives—and representatives from the entire animal kingdom! What amazing faith this man exhibited!

Go back to Genesis 6 and see some of the fascinating things that took place. God told Noah, "Make for yourself an ark of gopher wood; you shall make the ark with rooms, and shall cover it inside and out with pitch" (v. 14). That was a challenge to faith and obedience on an unprecedented scale. What would you do if God told you to build a 20,000-ton ship in the middle of the wilderness? Think about it. One of the greatest acts of obedience in the history of the world took place when Noah rolled up his sleeves and chopped down that first tree.

I can't resist a digression from our subject. The Hebrew word translated "pitch" is exactly the same word translated "atonement." It can be either. Leviticus 17:11 might read this way: "For the life of the flesh is in the blood, and I have given it to you on the altar to make atonement [to be pitch] for your souls; for it is the blood by reason of the life that makes atonement [serves as pitch]." In the ark of safety, the pitch kept the waters of judgment out. And the pitch in the life of believers is the blood of Christ, which secures us from any judgment. The pitch in the ark was what kept the water out, and the blood of Christ seals the believer from the flood of God's judgment.

The Size of the Ark

Genesis 6:15 gives us the dimensions of the ark: "This is how you shall make it: the length of the ark three hundred cubits, its breadth fifty cubits, and its height thirty cubits." God gave Noah a verbal blueprint. As you may know, there is quite a bit of variation in how much an ancient cubit measured, since it took as its standard the distance between a man's elbow and middle finger. In general terms, the dimensions of the ark would be about 450 feet long, seventy-five feet wide, and forty-five feet high—about the height of a four-story building. Since the ark had three decks, its total area was approximately 95,000 square feet. That would be more than twenty standard-sized basketball courts. Its size places it well within the category of large, steel, oceangoing vessels of our modern world. As far as we can tell, it was similar to a covered raft—shaped like a coffin—rather square and flatbottomed.

An instructor once gave a lecture to admirals at the U.S. Naval Academy. "For centuries," this man said, "men built ships in various proportions. But since British naval machinists found the formula for the battleship *Dreadnought*, all naval construction follows the proportions of *Dreadnought*, since they have been found to be scientifically perfect." Then he added, "The proportions of *Dreadnought* are exactly the same as the ark."

The Weather Forecast: Rain

"Behold, I, even I am bringing the flood of water upon the earth, to destroy all flesh in which is the breath of life, from under heaven; everything that is on the earth shall perish" (Genesis 6:17). That must have been difficult for Noah to understand. He had no concept of rain since it had never rained before (see Genesis 2:5). Instead, a mist from the earth continually watered the ground.

Many creation scientists believe the earth was surrounded by a vapor canopy. That would help explain the long life spans of those who lived before the Flood. Harmful rays of the sun did not penetrate this canopy; so the process of deterioration was greatly slowed down. When the canopy collapsed during the Flood

(Genesis 7:11), the protection was removed, and man's life span immediately began decreasing.

More Than a Century of Fruitless Preaching

When God first told Noah the Flood was coming, it was still a long way off—120 years, in fact (Genesis 6:3). Noah could easily have rationalized and taken his task casually. If he were a procrastinator, the ark might never have been built. Moreover, during those long years Noah preached. He preached earnestly and unrelentingly, although no one believed him. As a preacher myself, I know that must have been hard to take. Yet Noah kept right on giving out the message.

Perhaps as the years wore on, Noah began to question. He may have begun to think, *I wonder if there's something wrong with me. I've gone over this sermon many, many times, and no one buys it.* You can well imagine what this man of obedience must have endured as he pounded and preached.

People passing by would point to him, touch their heads, and say, "There's that crazy Noah."

Perhaps he would think, *Even if the Flood does come, how is this monster going to float—especially with all the different animals in it? It has no anchor, no mast, no steering, no rudder, no sail— not much of anything except floor space.* But through it all, Noah believed God and obeyed Him.

God Establishes His Covenant

In Genesis 6:18 God made this promise to Noah: "But I will establish My covenant with you; and you shall enter the ark—you and your sons and your wife, and your sons' wives with you." That promise, like all God's promises, had its foundation in God's grace (Genesis 6:8). Grace is strictly God's to give to whom He will. Noah was a sinner, like all men. In fact, he fell into gross sin after the Flood (Genesis 9:21). God extended grace to Noah simply because He desired to do so. It pleased the Lord to be gracious to Noah—to spare him and to make a covenant with him.

Genesis 6:19-21 records God's further instructions to Noah:

"And of every living thing of all flesh, you shall bring two of every kind into the ark, to keep them alive with you; they shall be male and female. Of the birds after their kind, and of the animals after their kind, of every creeping thing of the ground after its kind, two of every kind will come to you to keep them alive. As for you, take for yourself some of all food which is edible, and gather it to yourself; and it shall be for food for you and for them."

God was in essence saying, "After you've built this boat, I want you to get the animals into it and provide for their care."

Imagine, if you can, the day this was all fulfilled. Noah just sat at the gangplank, waiting for all those animals to come in from everywhere. He didn't have to go out and round them up; they just came. There is no way to explain that fact other than that God was herding them into this big boat.

It's been calculated from a spatial standpoint that the ark could easily have handled 7,000 species of animals. That's quite a number! It doesn't necessarily mean two of every animal in the world, since one basic species can generate a wide range of varieties. All horses, for instance, whether Shetland ponies, racing horses, draft animals, or whatever, are descended from one common ancestor. Two cows could well have represented the whole bovine family. So it is very likely that the species were limited. It is within reason to assume there was plenty of room for every species on board. It has been estimated that there is a total of about 2,500 animal species—the average size being that of a cat, which would require less than two square feet of living space. So from a logistical standpoint it was no problem to get the animals into the ark. But that still left the matter of the feeding and care of this great number of animals. Who would feed them? How would the sanitation problem be cared for? You can see the enormous problems of preparing to spend a year on that boat.

Total Obedience

Noah was a man of obedience; so he began to build. "Thus Noah did; according to all that God had commanded him, so he did"

(Genesis 6:22). What faith! Total obedience! How unlike most of us. God might want us to take responsibility for some ministry or to reach some person He brings into our lives, or He asks us to trust Him in a trial we're going through. How often we fail to obey God in such situations, let alone build an ark! We say we believe, but our faith is infinitesimal in relation to that of Noah. And some of us run out of patience very quickly. We think it's a major victory when we obey for a week. Noah obeyed for 120 years!

What were the grounds for his obedience? Nothing more than God's Word. He believed that God meant what He said about judgment and what He said about His promise. So Noah built the ark exactly as he was supposed to. He obeyed God to the letter. He didn't pick and choose his points of obedience. Some people want to believe God about His promises, but not about judgment; but we must believe both equally. Charles Spurgeon said:

> He who does not believe that God will punish sin, will not believe that God will pardon it through the atoning blood. . . . I charge you who profess to be the Lord's not to be unbelieving with regard to the terrible threatenings of God to the ungodly. Believe the threat, even though it should chill your blood; believe, though nature shrinks from the overwhelming doom; for, if you do not believe, the act of disbelieving God about one point will drive you to disbelieve him upon the other parts of revealed truth.[2]

So Noah believed God. He believed not only the promise of safety in the ark, but also in the imminent destruction of the world. He believed both. He believed God totally.

NOAH REBUKED THE WORLD

Noah believed God's Word and responded to it in obedient faith. That obedience on his part rebuked the world. Hebrews 11:7 tells us, "By faith Noah, being warned by God about things not yet seen, in reverence prepared an ark for the salvation of his household, by which he condemned the world."

Just how did Noah proclaim his message of condemnation to the world? By building an ark. That was his sermon. Every time a passerby saw him or heard him chop down a tree or looked up at him walking along with a plank on his back, that person heard or saw a sermon. And it was saying, "Judgment is coming. Judgment is coming. Judgment is coming." Yet not one person believed, even though Noah stayed at his task 120 long years.

Not even the carpenters assisting Noah accepted his message. Noah must have hired many men to help him and his sons because they alone could never have carried the massive timbers they used in the construction of the ark. But although these workers helped him build it, they were not saved by the ark. They took their weekly wages, then perished in the Flood. Likewise today people assist in building the church by their labor and by their talent. They work for self-satisfaction, the praise of men, or whatever. Jesus said of such people, "They have their reward in full" (Matthew 6:2, 5, 16). Their reward is an earthly one only. They are lost and will perish because they are not secure in Christ.

Was God being too severe with these laborers who worked with Noah on the ark? No. Genesis 6:5 tells us what kind of people they were: "Then the LORD saw that the wickedness of man was great on the earth, and that every intent of the thoughts of his heart was only evil continually." Each one was vile on the inside, and God saw it all. "For man looks at the outward appearance, but the LORD looks at the heart" (1 Samuel 16:7). God reads the heart.

But God's heart was also involved. "The LORD was sorry that He had made man on the earth, and He was grieved in His heart" (Genesis 6:6). Does that mean God changed His mind? Was He taken by surprise? Was He indicating that He had made a mistake in creating man? No. This is an anthropomorphism—a statement about God in human terminology. Scripture is conveying to us a sense of God's grief and sorrow at the state of the human race. From a human standpoint, it appears as if God had a change of heart, regretting that He had made man. But 1 Samuel 15:29 tells us, "The Glory of Israel will not lie or change His mind; for He is not a man that He should change His mind."

God's Judgment

God hadn't changed His mind or anything like that—it was mankind that had changed. All of humanity had grown so corrupt that God decided to erase the race. "The LORD said, 'I will blot out man whom I have created from the face of the land, from man to animals to creeping things and to birds of the sky; for I am sorry that I have made them'" (Genesis 6:7).

That was a radical solution to the problem. But the problem was worse than you might imagine. Much of the race had become a demonic aberration. When the Bible says that the sons of God cohabited with the daughters of men (Genesis 6:2), I believe the reference applies to fallen angels. Demons having sexual relations with women had evidently produced a grotesque race (the Nephilim, Genesis 6:4) that was partly demonic. So God decided to wipe out the entire race—except for Noah and his family—in a worldwide, catastrophic judgment.

Was God too severe? Was this the end of His mercy? No; the fact that God's patience will end, the fact that He will ultimately judge—this is the only hope for a sin-cursed world. If God hadn't acted to destroy, men would have had to live in a world of eternal sin and violence. And that would be unthinkable. We ought to be thankful that sin gets judged. God is holy and just, and He must set things right. But judgment comes only after God's great patience.

That God should judge a sinful world is neither unfair nor too severe. In fact, the remarkable thing about God's actions here is His mercy in preserving the race at all. If God had simply wiped out everyone, including Noah and his family, that would have been the end of sinful humanity on the earth. God could have restored earth to the perfect world He created. But because He is a God of mercy, He desires to redeem fallen mankind. So He preserved the race in the midst of this terrible judgment.

Humanity's Rejection

Every person has enough knowledge of God so that he is without excuse (Romans 1:19, 20). From the time of Adam and Eve, God had promised a Redeemer (Genesis 3:15). From that time on, the expiatory sacrificial system was in effect. Mankind knew how to come to God. Adam lived 930 years and perhaps spent most of that time telling his offspring the truth about what sin had done to him and to the world. The preaching of Enoch served as a warning (Jude 14, 15), as did the ministry of Noah. But there came a time when the Spirit of God no longer tried to make the case. The people knew the truth, but they had stubbornly rejected it. Noah's life of obedience stood out in bold relief as an open rebuke to the men of his time.

Is that very different from our own day? Our Lord said, "For the coming of the Son of Man will be just like the days of Noah" (Matthew 24:37). Noah preached, and people laughed, just as people now snicker at the proclamation of the Gospel. But in Noah's day a remnant found grace, and today, too, people are being saved by the grace of God—saved not from a judgment of water, but from a judgment of eternal fire. God needs more men and women like Noah—those who will obey God no matter how bizarre or difficult His commands may seem.

THE MOTIVATION FOR OBEDIENCE

As great an example as Noah was, however, we can't leave this subject of obedience without updating it by a New Testament concept. This will round out our understanding of obedience as a key to growth. Remember that we began this chapter by suggesting that one way to tell whether or not a person was a genuine Christian or a counterfeit Christian was the measure of that person's obedience. But what is the motivating force of obedience? What kind of obedience is it? Let's see if we can find out from the book of 1 John.

"By this we know that we have come to know Him, if we keep His commandments" (1 John 2:3). The word "keep" in that verse carries the idea of watchful, observant obedience. It is not speaking of an obedience in response to force or pressure. We do not say,

"Well, I have to obey because if I don't, I'll get whacked by the divine hammer." No, it isn't like that at all. It's an obedience that responds out of pure love for one's Master.

Alford's Greek Testament defines the Greek word translated "keep" as "to watch or guard or to keep, as some precious thing." The true Christian demonstrates that he knows God by the great desire of his heart to guard obedience. The habitual, moment-by-moment safeguarding of the Word of God in a spirit of obedience is the sign of a mature Christian. When people claim to be Christians, yet live any way they want, in complete disregard for God's commandments, they undermine their own testimony and put their claim of knowing Christ in doubt.

The word that John uses here for "commandments" is also significant. In the book of 1 John, the apostle uses the word *entole* at least fourteen times, referring to the precepts of Christ. But in his Gospel, when John speaks of the Law of Moses, he uses a different word—*nomos*. In his first epistle John wants to emphasize the precepts of Christ rather than the Law of Moses. If we have a spirit of obedience toward the safeguarding of the precepts of Christ, a consuming desire that they be honored, and a determination to obey them, that constitutes continuing experiential proof that we have come to the knowledge of God and the Lord Jesus Christ.

When a person becomes a Christian, he openly acknowledges that Jesus is his Lord. And if he sincerely enthrones Christ, he will gladly submit to His authority. Obedience is a foregone conclusion. If a person says to Jesus, "You are Lord!" that settles the question. Thus those who continue to keep His commandments are the ones who really know God and are assured of it.

TWO KINDS OF OBEDIENCE

But what if we try to be obedient and fail? Are we condemned? I have struggled with this problem so long, I think I can help you understand it. We must distinguish between *legal* obedience and *gracious* obedience. Legal obedience is the result of fleshly effort. Legal obedience demands an absolute, perfect obedience without a single failure. If you violate God's Law even once, the penalty is death. That is the pain and failure of legal obedience.

But there is such a thing as gracious obedience. The terminology gives a clue about how the two kinds of obedience differ. Gracious obedience is a loving and sincere spirit of obedience motivated by God's grace to us. Though often defective, that obedience is nevertheless accepted by God, for its blemishes are blotted out by the blood of Jesus Christ.

See the difference? With fleshly, human effort, obedience must be perfect to be of any value. With divine grace, God looks at the heart, not at the works. I'm glad, aren't you? If God were measuring me on legal obedience, I would spend eternity in hell. But God looks at me and says in effect, "MacArthur, with all your defects, you have a heart that desires to be obedient to Me. You have a spirit that wills to submit to My Lordship, even though you frequently fail."

That is the point of the cross of Christ. Jesus died, bearing the full penalty for our sins and failings, so that His blood can cover whatever is defective in our day-to-day obedience. It is far better to be under gracious obedience than under legal obedience.

Lest anyone get the wrong idea, let me illustrate. Did the disciples always obey God? Of course they didn't. Take Peter, for example, or James or John. All failed the Lord and made mistakes, being sinful men. Yet of them all Jesus could say to the Father, "They have kept Your word" (John 17:6). Had they? Consistently? They would have blushed at the very suggestion. Was Jesus measuring them by an absolute Mosaic legal obedience, or was He measuring their obedient spirits? You know the answer. Their propensity, their desire, their determination to submit to Jesus Christ—that's what Jesus measured, and He covered their defects with His shed blood.

God's standard of holiness is still absolute perfection, but He has graciously made provision for our inevitable failures. If we do something wrong or fail, He doesn't say we are finished and no longer Christians. God is looking at the constant flow of a heart that has in it the spirit of obedience. The true Christian has a desire to submit to Jesus Christ, even though he cannot always make that desire come to pass. But God reads and accepts it.

Such obedience is based not on law but on love, not on fear but on friendship. Several verses in John point this out. As Jesus was telling of His imminent return to heaven, He did not say, "Now keep My commandments or else." Rather He said, "He who has my commandments and keeps them is the one who loves Me" (John 14:21). So we obey not because we fear but because we love.

Non-Christians, of course, know nothing of this gracious obedience. Instead of submitting themselves to the lordship of Christ, they go about trying to crank out righteousness of their own and by that act are damning themselves under legal obedience. "They profess to know God, but by their deeds they deny Him" (Titus 1:16). They may make a profession of knowing God, but unlike Noah, their works don't back them up. At the Great White Throne judgment, many people are going to say, "Lord, Lord, have we not done wonderful works in Your name?" But Jesus will answer, "Depart from Me, I never knew you" (see Matthew 7:21-23).

There is no true knowledge of Christ that does not result in a spirit of gracious obedience.

THE PATTERN OF OBEDIENCE

We have, then, the principle that it is possible to identify a Christian because of his obedience. Now let's go on to the *pattern* of obedience. By pattern I mean something you can trace. First John 2:6 tells us, "The one who says he abides in Him ought himself to walk in the same manner as He walked." The word "abides" is equivalent in John's writings to expressions like "knowing Him," "walking in the light," "being in fellowship." All those terms indicate salvation. The point is that if you declare you are a Christian, you ought to show a pattern of walking in the same manner as He walked.

You might say, "Oh, it was bad enough that we had to keep His commandments. Now we have to walk like Him. I can't do it!" Well, the verse does not say that every aspect of our walk will be exactly like Him, but that we will walk in the same manner. Christ is our pattern. We are to move toward the likeness of Christ. We ought to live as He lived. Obedience moves us toward Christlikeness.

Take a couple of specifics. Philippians 2:8 tells us about Jesus: "Being found in appearance as a man, He humbled Himself by becoming obedient to the point of death, even death on a cross." Jesus was in the form of God, but He did not insist on hanging on to that glory and privilege. Instead, he was willing to lay it aside temporarily and humble Himself. That is the greatest illustration of humility ever. And that is our pattern to follow.

Note that this passage also speaks of Christ's obedience. Our Lord was obedient in everything. He paid His taxes. He obeyed the Mosaic Law to the very letter. He obeyed the ceremonial law. He obeyed the special divine stipulations of His messiahship. John's Gospel makes this point very clear. Jesus said, "For I have come down from heaven, not to do My own will, but the will of Him who sent Me" (John 6:38). His entire attitude was marked by a spirit of obedience. Again, "[The Father] has not left Me alone, for I always do the things that are pleasing to Him" (John 8:29). And in John 14:31: "I do exactly as the Father commanded Me." Again, obedience. Christ set the pattern. His loving obedience, then, becomes the very thing that we are to trace our lives after.

This chapter began with a reference to a man known as the Great Impostor. One day many years ago Ferdinand Waldo Demara, Jr., came into my dad's study and began to talk about Christianity. My preacher-father handed him a multivolume systematic theology— just as a starter. Demara devoured it in very short order. Ultimately he became a Christian—not a fake one but a genuine believer.

Whether or not you realize it, people are looking at your life all the time. They are hearing the sermon your life proclaims. "Thus Noah did; according to all that God had commanded him, so he did" (Genesis 6:22). Will the same be said of you? You grow to be like Christ while you obey.

5

THE FILLING OF
THE SPIRIT

Unlocking the Power Plant

Many years ago oil was discovered on Native American land in Oklahoma. The local tribe became instantly wealthy. A horde of unscrupulous businessmen descended on them, hawking everything from worthless trinkets to expensive luxury items, wanting to take advantage of the people before they fully understood the value of their money.

One of the tribesmen purchased a Rolls Royce. He drove it around for a week or so, but when it ran out of gasoline he assumed it was broken or that he had worn it out. Not wanting to lose face, he announced he was weary of it anyway and didn't want it anymore. One of his friends claimed the discarded automobile, removed the engine to reduce the car's weight, then hitched a team of horses to it. The horse-drawn Rolls Royce was his means of transportation for years.

Many people try to live the Christian life the same way. Misunderstanding the Holy Spirit's power, they seek other means to energize their spiritual lives. They try to generate power from within themselves or enlist the aid of some kind of support group or look for other sources of energy—everything but the one power source God intended: His indwelling Spirit.

As Christians, we know we are to be different from the world. We are instructed to love one another, to obey the Lord, to pray for our needs, to live holy lives, to walk in the light, and to be wise. But we simply cannot do those things in our own strength and energy. We must be filled with and controlled by the Holy Spirit. He is the only fuel, the only energizing resource, that God has provided for practical Christian living. To try to function without the Holy Spirit is like owning an oil well and not understanding that what it produces is necessary to make your car run.

A CONTRAST

Ephesians 5 is the key New Testament passage on being filled with the Holy Spirit. Verse 18 says, "Do not get drunk with wine, for that is dissipation, but be filled with the Spirit."

All people like to be happy—to be exhilarated with joy, to feel good, and to be on top of everything. There is nothing wrong with that. The Bible says there is a time to laugh. Scripture talks about shouting for joy and good tidings of great joy. It refers to joy unspeakable and full of glory. God wants joyous, excited, happy, and uplifted people. The problem lies in how our happiness is generated. Some people seek artificially induced bliss. You might expect in our modern world (where so much is artificial) that someone would get the idea of brewing joy and placing it in a bottle. And that is exactly what has been done! Today we have millions of Americans frantically seeking artificial joy at the bottom of a bottle.

Drunkenness, of course, occurs in all countries and cultures. The whole world faces a major epidemic of alcoholism. I once visited the jungles of Ecuador and had to avoid hitting drunk Indians on the road. Go to remote parts of Africa, and you will see that even the most primitive tribes have something intoxicating to drink. In Russia, alcoholism has developed into a national crisis. All over the world, people unable to find real happiness look for it in a drunken stupor. But all they find is a cheap, false, damning, artificial substitute for real joy.

In first-century times water was usually impure; so people mixed their drinking water with a little wine, which killed the dangerous amoebas. The resulting beverage was hardly intoxicating.

The alcohol content was so low, one would have to drink gallons of the stuff to get drunk. Undiluted, unmixed wine, however—called "strong drink" in Scripture—was imbibed by people who wanted to get high. Naturally, a Christian who drank wine as a daily part of his life would easily feel tempted toward drunkenness. The Bible repeatedly calls drunkenness a sin and warns against it. For example, Paul excluded those who were given too much wine from being elders or deacons in the church (1 Timothy 3:3, 8). Proverbs is filled with prohibitions against drunkenness.

What about wine in today's society? Should Christians drink at all? Some believers say, "Well, I don't get drunk. I only drink a little. Isn't that okay?" This actually is beyond the scope of our topic, but let me give what I have called "The Christian's wine list"—five key questions that can help us determine whether we as Christians should drink alcoholic beverages.

> • *Will it be habit-forming?* Paul said, "All things are lawful for me, but not all things are profitable. All things are lawful for me, but I will not be mastered by anything" (1 Corinthians 6:12).
> • *Will it lead to dissipation?* Scripture calls drunkenness dissipation or excess (Ephesians 5:18).
> • *Will it offend a weaker brother?* If another believer follows my example and falls into sin, then I have been the occasion for his stumbling (Romans 14:21).
> • *Will it harm my Christian testimony?* Someone may look at me and think less of my Christian testimony because of what I do (Romans 14:16).
> • *Am I certain that it is right?* If not, I'd be partaking of a doubtful thing, and that would be sin (Romans 14:23).

If Christians are not to be drunk with wine, then where are they to get true joy and happiness? The answer is clear: "Be filled with the Spirit" (Ephesians 5:18). Our thrills, our exhilaration, and our happiness are to result from being filled with the Spirit, not from being filled with wine.

The language in that verse may seem a little shocking. It sounds as if Paul is saying we should be drunk with the Holy Spirit. That is extraordinary imagery, but the Bible repeats it in several places. In Luke 1:15, for example, in the prophecy regarding the birth of John the Baptist, we learn that he "will drink no wine or liquor; and he will be filled with the Holy Spirit, while yet in his mother's womb." In other words, John would get his joy and motivating power—his fuel—not out of a bottle but through the filling of the Spirit of God.

How about Acts 2, which records the coming of the Holy Spirit upon the disciples at Pentecost? When the disciples went out and began to proclaim God's message, the unbelievers standing around said that these Christians were full of new wine (v. 13). They were suggesting that for anyone to be so happy, so jubilant, and so extroverted, they must be drunk. But Peter set them straight and insisted that instead of wine, it was the Holy Spirit at work (vv. 15-18).

Here's the idea: Being filled with the Holy Spirit results in behavior marked by joy, boldness, and a lack of inhibition. Similarly a meek, mild person can become just the opposite when he gets drunk. His personality may appear to change under the influence of alcohol. He becomes uninhibited. He doesn't seem to care what people think about him. He abandons himself to the effects of drink. Paul speaks of precisely the same kind of influence in those whom God fills with the Holy Spirit. They become completely abandoned to His control. The same kind of exhilaration and joy that so many people seek artificially in wine fills them.

Nevertheless, Paul is actually making a contrast, not a comparison, between wine and the Holy Spirit. Wine controls a person completely but works evil in the person's heart and life. The Holy Spirit also controls completely, but He empowers the person unto true righteousness. The Holy Spirit's controlling influence provides divine fuel for a different, free, uninhibited life lived for God's glory. It is the exact opposite of a life controlled by drunkenness.

THE COMMAND

Ephesians 5:18 also gives us a command: "Be filled with the Spirit." What does it mean to be Spirit-filled? First, let me point out something basic and exciting. Every Christian possesses the Holy

Spirit. Paul asked, "Do you not know that your body is a temple of the Holy Spirit who is in you?" (1 Corinthians 6:19). If you are a believer, the Spirit lives within you! "If anyone does not have the Spirit of Christ, he does not belong to Him" (Romans 8:9). So all believers possess the Spirit. You do not have to ask for the Spirit. He is in you and has been since the time of your salvation.

Paul never says, "Be indwelt by the Spirit." The believer is already indwelt. Paul never says, "Be baptized in the Spirit." The believer was baptized into the body of Christ at the moment of his conversion (1 Corinthians 12:13). Paul never says, "Be sealed with the Spirit." The believer is already sealed. Your possession of the Spirit, your indwelling by the Spirit, your baptism by the Spirit, your sealing by the Spirit—all those things were accomplished at your salvation.

What Paul is saying here, literally, is, "Be continually letting the Spirit of God, who is already in you, fill you." The Greek verb means "be continually filled" or "be kept filled." The Greek verb tense is one of continuous action. Paul is not speaking of a second work of grace. Being filled with the Spirit is not a onetime experience, a step up to a higher level of spirituality. Being Spirit-filled simply means continually letting the Spirit of God, who is already in you, control you.

This truth can be seen clearly in the book of Acts. Start with chapter 4 and study through chapter 13. You will repeatedly read that the same disciples were filled here, filled there, filled on this circumstance and on that. We, too, need to be filled again and again as we yield control to the Holy Spirit. We never come to the place where we can say, "Well, I have the filling, so now I'm set." The filling of the Holy Spirit is a continuous experience. We may be filled today, but tomorrow is a new opportunity.

UNDER THE INFLUENCE

We need to clarify precisely what is meant by "filled." Some might hold the idea that it is like dumping something into a glass to fill it up. But that's not a good parallel. Let me give a better illustration from one of my older books.

A Fizzie is a small tablet used to make a soft drink; it's sort of a flavored Alka-Seltzer. Put it in a glass of water and its flavor releases throughout the water. This concentrated, compact power pill is no good as long as it sits on the bottom of the glass. It has to release its energy to fill the glass, and then it turns the water into something new. If it is a grape Fizzie, you get a glass of grape drink. The flavor of the tablet determines the flavor of the water.

In a measure, that pictures how the Spirit of God operates in a human life. He is in the Christian all the time as a compact, concentrated, powerful force of divine energy. The question is, has He ever been able to release that power, to fill your life so that you can become what He is? A Christian not yielded to the Spirit of God does not manifest the Christ-life. The Spirit of God has to permeate a life if that life is to radiate Him.

We cannot do anything apart from being filled with the Spirit.

I have a glove. I say to the glove, "Play the piano," what does the glove do? Nothing. The glove cannot play the piano. But if I put my hand in the glove and play the piano, what happens? Music! But if I put my hand in a glove, the glove moves. The glove does not get pious and say, "Oh, hand, show me the way to go." It does not say anything; it just goes. Spirit-filled people do not stumble and mumble around trying to find out what God wants. They just go!

People often ask, "How do I know my spiritual gift?" The best way is to live a Spirit-filled life, see what God does through you, look back in retrospect and say, "Oh, that's what I do when God has control of me. Apparently, that is my gift." There is no need to get analytical. The whole point is that we need the Spirit of God to be released in our lives. This is simply a matter of decisions. When you get up in the morning, you decide what you are going to wear. Next you decide what you are going to eat for breakfast. And so it goes through the day— one decision after another. The Spirit-filled life is yielding every decision to the control of the Spirit.[1]

In a sense, that is how the Holy Spirit fills the Christian's life. He is already there, ready to explode with His power. The question is not whether He's there, but rather, whether His power fills our lives so that He controls all that we say, think, and do. Being filled with the Spirit means having the Holy Spirit released to permeate your life—to fill you in every dimension so that you become like Him.

To understand better what it means to be filled with the Holy Spirit, consider some New Testament passages that refer to other types of filling. In John 16:6, for example, after Jesus told His disciples that He was going away, they were filled with sorrow; that is, they were consumed with sorrow. In Luke 6:11, after Jesus presented His claims as Messiah, the people were "filled with rage." In other words, they were totally captured by the feeling of rage. Acts 5:3 tells us that Satan filled Ananias' heart, meaning Ananias was overwhelmed by the power of the evil one. So we see that the word *filled* signifies being totally captive to a particular emotion, power, or influence.

In Acts 4:31 we read that when the church "had prayed, the place where they had gathered together was shaken, and they were all filled with the Holy Spirit, and began to speak the word of God with boldness." They were consumed with the Spirit of God—with the joy, the power, and the influence of the Holy Spirit. As a result they could move out uninhibited, unbridled by their own egos, totally self-abandoned and thus could communicate Jesus Christ boldly.

The same can be true of us. We can be so captive to the Holy Spirit that we are utterly controlled by Him. His influence then crowds out our usual fears and other emotions. The result is boldness and a great exhilaration, a thrilling happiness beyond any other—joy upon joy—because He controls and captures every part of us.

THE MEANS: SURRENDER

To be filled with the Holy Spirit means to be totally under His influence. How does that happen? It is simply a matter of surrendering your will, your mind, your body, your time, your talents, your treasures—every area of your life—to the control of the Holy Spirit. It is saying, "I want the Spirit of God to be the overwhelming, controlling influence in my life."

The context of Ephesians 5:18 shows exactly what it means to be Spirit-filled. The apostle Paul goes on to list some of the things that a person who is filled with the Spirit does. A Spirit-filled person sings songs. The Spirit-filled wife submits to her husband. The Spirit-filled husband loves his wife. Spirit-filled children obey their parents. A Spirit-filled father does not provoke his children to wrath. A Spirit-filled employer is fair with his employees. All those are manifestations of the Spirit-filled life.

Now check Colossians 3:16: "Let the word of Christ richly dwell within you." What happens when that occurs? The very same thing that happens when you are filled with the Spirit (see vv. 16-23). Therefore, being filled with the Spirit is exactly the same thing as letting the Word of Christ dwell in you richly. They must be equal, for they produce exactly the same phenomena.

Now let's go one step further for an additional comparison. To be Spirit-filled is to be Christ-conscious. It is practically the same thing as being deeply, richly involved in all that Jesus Christ is and what is said about Him. The truth Jesus spoke and the truth taught about Him should govern every deed, every word, every internal drive, every hidden motive, and every desire of your heart. And as you study the Word of God, as you dwell in His Word, as it dwells in you richly, you become Christ-centered, you become Christ-conscious. That is the same as being Spirit-filled.

To put it another way, being filled with the Spirit means living every moment as if you are standing in the presence of Jesus Christ. You can get up in the morning and in your heart say, "Good morning, Lord. It's Your day, and I just want You to keep reminding me all day that You are right beside me." What is more practical than that? When Satan or his agents come around to tempt you, you can say, "Christ, I know You are in me. Empower me! Rebuke Satan and his powers. Lord, I'm being tempted, and I need Your strength right now!"

Being Spirit-filled also gives practical help in making decisions. "Lord, I don't know which way to go. I have two choices, two paths. Show me the way, Lord." If you are really Christ-conscious, you just let Him guide your choices as you move through the day.

Have you learned to live in a Christ-conscious way? Do you habitually think of Jesus and acknowledge His presence in your life? That is the same as being Spirit-filled. Check out 2 Corinthians 3:18: "But we all, with unveiled face, beholding as in a mirror the glory of the Lord, are being transformed into the same image from glory to glory, just as from the Lord, the Spirit." You see, if you gaze at the Lord Jesus Christ, the Spirit will remake you into His glorious image! That's the ultimate in spiritual growth and can occur only when you are totally absorbed in Him!

SINGING AND MAKING MELODY

We've referred repeatedly to the joy that comes with being Spirit-filled. That joy is an inevitable consequence of the Spirit's control in a person's life. Ephesians 5:19 shows the consequence of a Spirit-filled life: "speaking to one another in psalms and hymns and spiritual songs, singing and making melody with your heart to the Lord."

It doesn't matter whether you sing well aloud. The point is that you can make melody in your heart. Do you know what it is to have a song in your heart? If you are filled with the Spirit, you can't help singing. That's not just my opinion; the Bible says so. How could it be otherwise if you have the joy and the exhilaration of the Spirit? As Spirit-filled Christians, we sing.

To whom do we sing? Our verse says, "to one another." In the church we sing to one another. Sometimes the choir sings to us, and sometimes we all sing together. Sometimes someone sings a solo. All of us sing because of the joy produced by the filling of the Spirit. Our songs are a testimony to one another, not mere entertainment. We must be aware of the danger of singing artificially—performing as a self-centered showcase and doing so for fleshly gratification rather than out of the joy of a Spirit-filled life. A performance that does not express the Spirit-filled life is sin because it stems from the desire for self-glory.

In addition to singing to one another, we're to sing "to the

Lord." Do you know that the Lord loves to hear you sing when you give expression to the joy of the Spirit? Music is the language of the emotions. How wonderful to express your innermost self directly to the Savior! If this is not the true expression of a sincere heart and backed by a righteous life, God is not pleased (Amos 5:23, 24).

What are we supposed to sing? According to our verse, we sing "psalms"—songs drawn directly from Scripture. We also sing "hymns"—the kind the disciples sang in the upper room the night before our Lord suffered and died. And last, we sing "spiritual songs"—personal, emotional expressions of our testimony. The phrase "and making melody" is translated from the Greek word *psallo*, which literally means "to pluck the lyre." Evidently we can also express our joy with instruments. Whether instrumentally or vocally, however, our reason for musical expression is the overwhelming joy of the Holy Spirit that fills us.

GIVING THANKS

In addition to singing, there is a further consequence of being Spirit-filled: giving thanks. Ephesians 5:20 says, "always giving thanks for all things in the name of our Lord Jesus Christ to God, even the Father." Spirit-filled, God-conscious Christians give thanks for everything. We tend to be long on our demands—yes, even our complaints—but we are often too short on our thanksgivings.

That was not true of one singularly sunny and praise-filled leader among the early Christians—the apostle Paul. For him it can be said that gratitude was far more a matter of principle than emotion, far more an affair of duty than of ecstasy. Wherever Paul went, he wore "the mantle of praise" (Isaiah 61:3). Some people, if they ever wear thankfulness at all, wear it as a boutonniere. Not Paul! He wore gratitude as a full outfit. Praise was woven into the fabric of his life. And he wanted it to be so with his Christian brethren everywhere. So strong was his insistence on that point that he laid it down emphatically to the Christians in the Colossian church with a two-word imperative: "Be thankful" (Colossians 3:15).

In the story of the ten lepers whom Jesus healed, only one returned to give thanks (Luke 17:11-19). And today thanksgiving is still outnumbered at least nine to one—a pathetic minority.

Thanksgiving is not an act; it is an attitude. "Let the peace of Christ rule in your hearts, to which indeed you were called in one body; and be thankful" (Colossians 3:15). Gratitude fills the soul with the sunshine of God. Ingratitude keeps the soul's windows darkened, shutting out the light of God, turning life into a fog. For the Christian, every circumstance should be cause for thanksgiving. Like the prophet Habakkuk, you may not understand, but you praise God anyway.

Benjamin Franklin recorded of the first Thanksgiving holiday in the New World, "In a time of great despondency among the first settlers of New England, it was proposed in one of their assemblies to proclaim a fast. An old farmer rose, reviewed their mercies, and proposed that, instead of provoking heaven with their complaints, they appoint a thanksgiving." We might learn a great lesson from that! We tend to focus so often on our complaints, but we could give thanks for many things. Whatever our losses are here on this earth, we know that as Christians we shall someday receive our divine, eternal inheritance in glory—and for that we can always be thankful. Those things for which we are thankful ought to set the agenda in our prayer lives. That's an integral part of the Spirit-filled life.

Jesus said, "Your grief will be turned into joy" (John 16:20). He then used the example of a woman giving birth to a child. The pain is agonizing, but when the child is born, the joy is unequaled. For us the very event that causes sorrow will bring joy, and we should thank Him and rejoice in advance. The indwelling Spirit will produce that kind of thanksgiving in everyone whom He fills!

THINGS FOR WHICH TO BE THANKFUL

Scripture is replete with exhortations to be thankful. Here are some of the many things we can always be thankful for.

• *Gifts from God*—1 Timothy 4:3, 4: ". . . God has created [marriage and food] to be gratefully shared in by those who believe and know the truth. For everything created by God is good, and nothing is to be rejected if it is received with gratitude."

• *God's presence*—Psalm 75:1, 9: "We give thanks to You, O God, we give thanks, for Your name is near; men declare Your wondrous works. . . . But as for me, I will declare it forever; I will sing praises to the God of Jacob."

• *Salvation*—Romans 6:17: "But thanks be to God that though you were slaves of sin, you became obedient from the heart to that form of teaching to which you were committed."

• *Victory over death*—1 Corinthians 15:57: "But thanks be to God, who gives us the victory through our Lord Jesus Christ."

• *Victory in life*—2 Corinthians 2:14: "But thanks be to God, who always leads us in triumph in Christ, and manifests through us the sweet aroma of the knowledge of Him in every place."

• *Everything in general*—Philippians 4:6: "Be anxious for nothing, but in everything by prayer and supplication with thanksgiving let your requests be made known to God."

SPIRITUAL MATURITY

It is only possible in the Christian life to be either Spirit-controlled or dominated by the flesh. The apostle Paul contrasted spiritual people with carnal ones. All unbelievers are carnal; they have no other option. Believers, on the other hand, have the Holy Spirit living in them; it is their nature to be spiritual. But believers are sometimes influenced by the flesh and can behave in carnal ways. Growth toward Christ's likeness occurs only when we are spiritual, walking in the Spirit, filled by the Spirit. When we behave in a fleshly manner, we hinder our spiritual growth.

Paul wrote, "And I, brethren, could not speak to you as to spiritual men, but as to men of flesh, as to babes in Christ. I gave you milk to drink, not solid food; for you were not yet able to receive it. Indeed, even now you are not yet able" (1 Corinthians 3:1, 2). In other words, Paul could feed the Corinthians only the milk of the Word—the basic truths—because their carnality had stunted their spiritual growth. They lacked the spiritual teeth necessary to chew solid food. Growth can occur only when we allow the Spirit to control us.

Full maturity results only from being filled with the Spirit as a pattern of life. Fuel up, friend, and head for the prize—to be made like Christ.

6

CONFESSION

Unlocking the Chamber of Horrors

At the height of his power, King David committed a grievous sin. He would suffer the consequences of it for the rest of his life. What did he do? He became infatuated with the wife of one of his military officers—Bathsheba was her name. David accidentally saw her bathing on her rooftop one day, and he began to lust after her. Ultimately he made her pregnant while her husband was away fighting battles on David's behalf.

David tried desperately to hide his deed and finally decided the only way to solve his problem was by arranging for Bathsheba's husband—his friend—to lead a suicide squad into a battle against the Philistines. That's what happened, and the innocent man was killed. Conveniently forgetting his intrigue, David gave the man a military funeral and proceeded to marry the pregnant wife. God relates the whole story in 2 Samuel 11.

By his actions David had broken four of the Ten Commandments: He had coveted, he had stolen, he had committed adultery, and he had murdered. A man with any moral sense, especially a man who knows God, is going to feel troubled, even unnerved, by such sin. Guilt finally caught up with David, and he became obsessed with his sin. He could not get his sin out of his heart or mind, and he could not get it off his hands.

Psalm 51 records David's great outpouring of confession. There he prayed for four things. Sin had made him dirty, and he asked to be cleansed. Guilt had made him physically sick, and he asked to be healed. Iniquity had broken his joy with God, and he asked to be restored. He knew he had directly violated God's love and laws, and he asked for pardon and mercy.

The whole subject of confession of sin is much discussed today, and I think we need to see it in the biblical perspective. Confession is ever and always the pattern of the Christian's life. It constitutes one of the essential keys to spiritual growth.

THE CONSEQUENCES OF COVERING SIN

Christians today face the same dilemma that David faced: If we try to cover our sin, as David attempted to do for an entire year, we grieve the Holy Spirit. Confession is the only solution, but it requires that we abandon our pride. We have all fought this battle.

I can remember in my childhood confronting the matter head-on time after time. My mother would line up all four children against the wall and say, "All right, which one of you did it?" To admit or not to admit—that was the question! You know, of course, that this is a recurring issue all through life. Fortunately, I learned as a child that it never pays to try to cover your sin. Besides, it is futile. We can hide nothing from God.

What happens to the one who covers up, or tries to? For one thing, he will forfeit God's blessing on his life. That means very real and practical consequences. "He who conceals his transgressions will not prosper" (Proverbs 28:13). Physical illness may be another result of covering up. David testified, "When I kept silent about my sin, my body wasted away through my groaning all day long. For day and night Your hand was heavy upon me; my vitality was drained away as with the fever heat of summer" (Psalm 32:3, 4).

The one who covers his sin in this life is going to have it uncovered in the next, and whoever exposes it to God in this life shall never have it exposed again in the life to come. A day of judgment is coming. Jesus said, "There is nothing covered up that will not be revealed, and hidden that will not be known. Accordingly, whatever you have said in the dark will be heard in the light, and what you have whispered in the inner rooms will be proclaimed upon the housetops" (Luke 12:2, 3).

A day is coming in which there will be absolutely no secrets, in which the innermost secrets of every heart will be disclosed. For the godly, that day will be rewarding; for the ungodly, the disclosure will be damning. God will judge all sin that has been covered up; all sin that is hidden will be revealed. But the sin that is exposed in this life and cleansed by the blood of Christ need never be exposed again. "If we confess our sins, He is faithful and righteous to forgive us our sins and to cleanse us from all unrighteousness" (1 John 1:9). That which has been cleansed and forgiven will not be brought against us.

That's one of the marvelous promises of Scripture that Christians can claim. When we get to heaven, God will not show us our sins. He has removed them from us "as far as the east is from the west" (Psalm 103:12)—an immeasurable distance.

But unbelievers who attempt to cover their sins have no such promise. They face exposure and God's judgment. Revelation 20 says that Christ will open the books to disclose the sin of their lives; He will judge all their sin, and He will cast the guilty into the lake of fire.

Moreover, Christians who try to cover individual sins face exposure and loss of reward:

> *Each man's work will become evident; for the day will show it because it is to be revealed with fire, and the fire itself will test the quality of each man's work. If any man's work which he has built upon it remains, he will receive a reward. If any man's work is burned up, he will suffer loss; but he himself will be saved, yet so as through fire.*
>
> —1 CORINTHIANS 3:13-15

God judges sin so sternly because He is utterly holy. All sin is a personal offense against Him. Everyone who sins directly defies God. David acknowledged that when he said, "Against You, You only, I have sinned, and done what is evil in Your sight" (Psalm 51:4). David did not deny that he had committed sin against himself and his own body, as adultery certainly is (1 Corinthians 6:18). He was not denying that he had sinned against Bathsheba and her husband or that he had sinned against the whole nation of Israel by failing in such a way. But he recognized that all sin is first and foremost an affront to God.

Some people tend to look for a place to lay blame when they think they're confessing sin. Adam, for example, began his admission of disobedience by saying, "*The woman* whom You gave to be with me, she gave me from the tree, and I ate" (Genesis 3:12, emphasis added). Many counselors today actually advise people to search their pasts and identify wrongs done to them by parents, authority figures, and others. Supposedly that process helps a person understand his failures and releases him from hurt he causes to himself. The truth is, none of that is helpful at all in dealing with guilt; in fact, it usually only worsens the problem. True confession of sin is not just admitting that you did something wrong, but acknowledging that your sin was against God and in defiance of Him personally. To be spiritually healthy, we must deal not with the issue of the wrongs others have done to us, but the evil we have perpetrated against a holy God.

So the primary feature of confession is agreeing with God that we are helplessly guilty. In fact, the Greek word for confession is *homologeo*, which literally means "to say the same thing." When we confess our sin, we must agree with God about our sin. That is, we must see our sin as He sees it. "Lord, I have sinned. I agree with Your appraisal of me."

So confession is not just saying, "Yes, I did it! I did it!" It means full agreement with God. For that reason, true confession also involves repentance—turning away from the evil thought or action. You have not honestly confessed your sins until you have turned from them. If a person says, "I'm sorry, God. I confess" and then continues to practice his sin, he fools himself. Real confession includes a brokenness that inevitably leads to changes in behavior.

Perhaps we tend to confess our sin in a superficial way because we do not understand how God sees our sin. We need to understand more fully what Scripture means when it speaks of confession. A closer look at David's confession in Psalm 51 shows us three crucial elements of true confession: a right view of sin, a right view of God, and a right view of self.

A RIGHT VIEW OF SIN

What is a right view of sin? First, it is *a recognition that sin deserves judgment*. David prayed, "Be gracious to me, O God, according to Your lovingkindness; according to the greatness of Your compassion blot out my transgressions" (v. 1). The fact that David pleaded for mercy was an admission that he was guilty and unworthy of exoneration or acquittal. The possibility of mercy comes only after a guilty verdict has been rendered.

Do you think David was at risk by praying such a prayer? Do you think there was a chance he might not receive mercy? Then read Psalm 103 for great news! "The LORD is compassionate and gracious, slow to anger and abounding in lovingkindness. . . . For as high as the heavens are above the earth, so great is His lovingkindness toward those who fear Him. . . . But the lovingkindness of the LORD is from everlasting to everlasting on those who fear Him" (vv. 8, 11, 17). We find many examples in Scripture where God stayed His hand of judgment and extended mercy (see Ezra 9:13; Nehemiah 9:19; and Job 11:6).

Still, a plea for mercy presupposes that sin deserves harsh judgment. We dare not presume on God's mercy. Let us never forget that the penalty for sin is death.

A right view of sin also recognizes *an urgent need for cleansing*. David prayed, "Wash me thoroughly from my iniquity, and cleanse me from my sin" (Psalm 51:2). He wanted every dirty sin washed out of his life. Sin leaves a deep stain, and only a total cleansing will suffice. What is the cleansing agent? "The blood of Jesus His Son cleanses us from all sin" (1 John 1:7). Jesus' atoning work on the cross paid the penalty for our sin. His blood was shed on our behalf so that we might be washed clean from all our iniquities. Without that cleansing, we would be doomed to an eternity apart from God.

But because He died for us, we can be washed "whiter than snow" (Psalm 51:7) and will enter God's holy presence in total purity.

A third thing is crucial to a right view of sin—the matter of *accepting full responsibility* for it. David wrote, "For I know my transgressions, and my sin is ever before me" (v. 3). As we have noted, David did not blame anyone except himself. He says in effect, "God, I exonerate You. I myself have done this. I have sinned. You are justified; You are clear. I don't try to escape my accountability." When a person takes personal responsibility for his sin, he advances toward spiritual maturity.

Finally, a right view of sin recognizes that *we sin because it is our nature to do so*. Sin is no accident. Nor could we stop if we made a willful decision to do so. We are utterly given to sin as a way of life. David said, "Behold, I was brought forth in iniquity, and in sin my mother conceived me" (v. 5). Sin is passed on from generation to generation at the time of conception. All of us are born utterly depraved—that is, sinful in every aspect of our nature. "The wicked are estranged from the womb" (Psalm 58:3). From their earliest moments, people are all evil. They cannot help it; it is a part of human nature, passed down from Adam.

A RIGHT VIEW OF GOD

Not only does true confession demand a right view of sin, it also demands a right view of God. In Psalm 51, David cites several characteristics of God and draws practical applications from them. *God's holiness*, for example, requires "truth in the innermost being" (v. 6). That implies God is concerned not with external behavior but with the thoughts and motives of our hearts. Some people try to play games with God by carrying on a lot of external religious ritual. He is not impressed with that. God looks on the inside—at the heart.

David also referred to *God's authority over sin*: "Purify me with hyssop, and I shall be clean" (v. 7). David expressed his confidence that if God were to take care of his sin, He would do the job thoroughly. Some Christians do not believe God can change their sinful habits. He can, but it requires trust and confidence in the Lord's authority over the powers of evil. How often we fail to commit ourselves totally to Him for victory!

After holiness and authority, David recognized *God's compassion*: "Make me to hear joy and gladness, let the bones which You have broken rejoice" (v. 8). What did David mean by "the bones which You have broken"? As a shepherd, he knew very well that those who tend flocks sometimes have to break the leg of a wayward lamb to keep him from straying. While the wounded limb is healing, the shepherd has to carry the little lamb until the set bone has healed. After that, the sheep will follow the shepherd closely wherever he goes. David got the message: "Lord, I had my legs broken, but now I'm ready to follow You." He saw God's compassion even in His acts of chastisement.

David also recognized *God's mercy*. He knew God is a forgiving God, that He has both the power and the desire to pardon sin in those whose repentance is genuine. I can think of no better expression of this than that found in Micah 7:18: "Who is a God like You, who pardons iniquity and passes over the rebellious act of the remnant of His possession? He does not retain His anger forever, because He delights in unchanging love." David understood this aspect of God's character; it is crucial to a right view of God.

A RIGHT VIEW OF SELF

So true confession demands a right view of sin, a right view of God, and one thing more—a right view of self. Psalm 51 makes this plain. David came to recognize that he needed to turn from his awful sin and live a holy, godly life.

Why? First, *for the sake of sinners*. David knew that he had to be holy if he was to convert other sinners to God (v. 13). No one is going to listen to a man who has a sense of guilt eating away at him. Moreover, guilt locks a person's lips from giving testimony. Someone harboring personal guilt has nothing to say to others looking for relief from their sin. I'm sure many Christians find themselves silent because they cannot avow the righteousness of God while they know they conceal secret transgressions.

Second, we must be holy *for the sake of God*, who delights in "a broken and a contrite heart" (v. 17). Do you know that you can make God happy? You can—by being sensitive to sin in your own life and being broken before the Lord about it.

Finally, we must be holy *for the sake of the saints*. In verse 18 David prays for others. Back in a right relationship with God, he can now intercede for others. But he could not do that unless he first came to the point of purity in his own life.

To summarize, true confession can occur only when you see God for who He is, when you see sin for what it is, and when you see yourself for what you are—and what you are to be.

IS CONFESSION REQUIRED FOR FORGIVENESS?

Let me dispel a wrong idea that some people have regarding this matter of confession. When we say confession involves both agreement with God and repentance that leads to sorrow for sin, are we saying that we must beg God for forgiveness? The answer is an emphatic no. Why is that? Because God has forgiven the believer's sin already! When Jesus Christ died on the cross, He bore the sins of each believer—his past sins, his present sins, and his future sins. So we are not dealing with the matter of forgiveness when we talk about confession. Forgiveness occurred at the cross. First John 2:12 says, "Little children . . . your sins are forgiven you *for His name's sake*" (emphasis added). There is no unforgiven sin in my life. There's none in your life either if you are a Christian. God does not impute sin to His children. Colossians 2:13 states that God has forgiven us all our trespasses and has made us one with Christ.

On a television program dealing with religious themes, the host invited people to telephone with their spiritual questions. A woman called in and asked, "If I die or the Rapture occurs before I have a chance to confess all my sins, what will happen to me? I'm a Christian." The host responded, "You'll go to hell." Not so! The Christian's sins have all been forgiven. Christians have eternal life as a present possession. They are one with Christ. That is what the cross accomplished. Nothing and no one can separate God's children from Him (see Romans 8:32-39).

CLEAN! CLEAN!

The *why* of confession will be considered in the remainder of this chapter. I warn you—it is a very heavy sea we are sailing through, so grab the railing and hang on!

We have to tackle three vital words that describe every Christian, taking as our text 1 John 1:5—2:2. The first word is *cleansed*. "If we walk in the light as He Himself is in the light, we have fellowship with one another, and the blood of Jesus His Son cleanses us from all sin" (1:7).

That is a fantastic description of a Christian. The Greek word translated "walk" is in a present-tense subjunctive, which means it speaks of continuous, habitual action. John is giving us an index of our true character. We might translate the first part of the verse, "If you are habitually in the light." Who is in the light? The Christian who has been placed in the light—the Christian who is sharing God's light and life. If you are in Him, then it follows that you are dwelling in the light.

The fact that Christians are living in light is very clear in Scripture. God is light, and no darkness is in Him. We are in His light. That is an absolute. No believer in Christ can step out of the light. We might occasionally return to the deeds of darkness, but those deeds are contrary to our new nature. We dwell in the light.

From the intellectual side, light refers to truth (see John 12:35, 36, 46; Acts 26:18, 23; 2 Corinthians 4:4, 6). From the moral side, light refers to holiness or purity (see Romans 13:11-14; Ephesians 5:8-14; 1 John 2:8-11). God is truth and holiness, and no sin touches Him. And we are in Him. What a thought!

Since we are walking in the light, "we have fellowship with one another." You might think "one another" refers to other Christians, but it doesn't. It refers to God and us. That is not evident in the English text, but it is in the Greek. As you walk in the light, you have fellowship with God, and He has fellowship with you. The word *fellowship* means "partnership." You are partners with God, sharing common life.

What is the result of this? "The blood of Jesus His Son cleanses us from all sin." We touched on that issue a few pages back. It is worth looking at in greater depth here. "The blood" is the symbol of Christ's death. Peter wrote, "You were not redeemed with perishable things like silver or gold from your futile way of life inherited from your forefathers, but with precious blood, as of a lamb unblemished and spotless, the blood of Christ" (1 Peter 1:18, 19). The blood symbolizes the Savior's death. His blood that was shed is a constant provision for our cleansing. That is, Christ needed to die only once to save us from our sins forever. He doesn't need to pay the price every time we sin anew. That once-for-all atonement keeps on cleansing us from our sin.

Revelation 1:5 also speaks to this point: "To Him [Jesus] who loves us and released us from our sins by His blood." When Jesus paid the price for sin by shedding His blood, that blood became like a cleansing agent to wash our sins away. It is not that Jesus' blood itself had some magical or mystical quality, but that the giving of His life paid the penalty for our sin. The shedding of His blood was a graphic demonstration that His death was a sacrifice for our sins.

In the Old Testament sacrificial system, the blood of an animal sacrifice was literally sprinkled around the Temple, on the altar, and even applied to the sinner who brought the sacrifice. That blood identified the sinner with the atonement. In a similar way, Christ's atoning death applies to us only when we personally identify with Him. His blood is not literally sprinkled on us, but as we identify ourselves personally with His death, it is as if we were literally sprinkled with His blood. Thus, symbolically the Bible speaks of the blood as the cleansing agent for our sins.

THE CONDITION FOR OUR CLEANSING

Is there any condition attached to our cleansing? Only one. We are cleansed if we walk in the light. Walking in the light, as we have seen, means being a Christian. If you are a Christian, you have absolute, total, complete, and continuous cleansing from all sin. That's what 1 John 1:7 affirms. There is no condition for cleansing but being in the light.

"No, no, that's wrong," someone objects. "This verse implies that we ought to walk in the light. It's saying, 'All right, you Christians, if you'll just get in earnest and walk in the light, then you'll have fellowship and then you'll be cleansed.'"

That's a common misunderstanding of this passage. But if that interpretation were correct, this verse, in effect, would be saying, "Don't sin because if you do, you'll be in darkness." So let's read it that way: "If you don't sin, the blood of Jesus Christ will cleanse you from all sin." Well, that is not what we need. That would mean you could get cleansing only when you do not need it. What value is there in getting cleansed when you are already being good? The implication would be that cleansing and forgiveness are available only to those who don't sin.

Instead the verse means that if you and I are walking in God's light, when sin comes into our lives we are nevertheless children of light, and sin is constantly cleansed from us because no darkness can invade God's light. So God continually cleanses and cleanses and cleanses us because of the sacrifice of Christ.

That's exciting! We don't have even one uncleansed sin on our accounts! Instead of being guilty and defiled, we are constantly cleansed. The moment some sin appears, we are cleansed because we are in the light. There is no darkness in Christ, and Christ keeps us pure.

Ephesians 1:7 tells us that we receive from Christ "redemption through His blood, the forgiveness of our trespasses, according to the riches of His grace." How complete is our forgiveness? "According to the riches of His grace." And Hebrews 10:14 reminds us that the offering of Christ "perfected for all time those who are sanctified." One offering—His death on the cross—led to our total cleansing, not just for one time, but for eternity.

I am fit to enter God's holy presence. I am going nonstop to glory! Christians are always in the light, always in the fellowship, and always cleansed. That's marvelous!

Let me give you an idea of how this works. On the occasion that our Lord washed the disciples' feet, Peter was offended that his Lord would stoop to such a lowly task. He said to Jesus, "Never shall You wash my feet!" (John 13:8). Peter's pride was offended. Washing feet was a servant's task. None of the disciples were willing to do it; so Jesus Himself had taken the basin and towel and was washing His own disciples' feet. This was an unheard-of role reversal—the Master was washing His disciples' feet.

Jesus answered, "If I do not wash you, you have no part with Me" (v. 8).

Peter, who seemed to have a knack for saying the wrong thing, came back with enthusiasm: "Lord, then wash not only my feet, but also my hands and my head" (v. 9).

"Jesus said to him, 'He who has bathed needs only to wash his feet, but is completely clean; and you are clean'" (v. 10). Someone who has had a bath is clean. In the first century, as people walked along the dusty road, their feet usually got dirty. They couldn't take a bath every time they walked someplace; so people commonly washed their feet. It was a touch-up, not a full cleansing.

Jesus was referring to a similar phenomenon in the spiritual realm. He was saying, "Once you have been cleansed with My blood, all sin has been forgiven. Only the dust of the world needs to be washed off your feet, and I will continue to do that. You don't need another bath."

That wonderfully pictures the positional cleansing and holiness of the Christian at salvation and gives us the promise that Jesus will continue to keep us clean every day as we walk through the world. We do not need to be saved over and over again. Salvation is a once-for-all transaction. It cannot be repeated.

CONFESSION IS GOOD FOR THE SOUL

If the first word that describes believers is *cleansed*, the second is *confessing*. "If we confess our sins, He is faithful and righteous to forgive us our sins and to cleanse us from all unrighteousness" (v. 9).

I have pointed out that there was no condition for cleansing in verse 7, but now we are at verse 9. You see, verse 7 looks at the matter from God's side, and verse 9 looks at it from our side. "Well, there you are!" someone might say, digging an elbow into my ribs. "You just said Christ takes care of our sins unconditionally, and now this verse says, 'if we confess.' So there is a condition after all!"

No, not really. This is not a *condition* for cleansing, but a *characteristic* of those who are being cleansed. Let me show you what I mean. God forgives and cleanses because of the death of Christ. God does this instantly, but He does it only for the people who are agreeing with Him about their sin. We could read 1 John 1:9 this way: "If we are the ones confessing our sins, He is faithful to forgive our sins." Who are the ones who are confessing? Christians. Do you see it? This verse is not saying, "You must confess or I will not forgive!" It says, in effect, that God constantly, habitually, forever cleanses the sins of the ones who are confessing. That is just another definition of a Christian. A Christian is someone who agrees with God that he is a sinner. So the ones who are admitting that they are sinners are the ones who are being cleansed.

Notice also that this verse says God is "faithful" in this forgiveness. He is faithful because He promised that He would cleanse and forgive. He promised He would be merciful to the one who confesses (Proverbs 28:13). In Jeremiah 31:34 He said, "I will forgive their iniquity, and their sin I will remember no more." So God is faithful because He does what He promised.

But our text adds that God is "righteous" or just in doing this. How could God possibly be just in forgiving sin? Doesn't justice demand rather that sin be punished? Yes, but Jesus Christ paid the penalty, and in doing that He satisfied God's justice. Romans 3:23-26 tells us that our Lord was crucified in order to display the justice of God, "so that He would be just and the justifier of the one who has faith in Jesus" (v. 26). The way God designed salvation, He can both justify sinners and remain just Himself.

Often a look at the original language illumines a difficult point. When 1 John 1:9 speaks of forgiving, the word used is in a tense that signifies a single, definite, onetime act rather than continuous action. John is not saying that Christians might live in continuous, unbroken sin. He is speaking of exceptional, occasional, sporadic acts of sin in the Christian's life. Those do occur, and they need to be confessed.

The Greek word translated "confess" in this verse appears in the continuing present tense. It refers to a continual confession of sins. This is not a one-time act. It is an ongoing attitude of agreeing with God concerning our sins. So the confession of a genuine believer is continual and habitual. God keeps forgiving the ones who are confessing—the ones agreeing with Him that they are sinners. So the continuous habit of their lives is to be acknowledging before God that they are sinners. In doing this, a confessor shows himself to be one who is truly forgiven—a true Christian—in contrast to the non-Christian, whose habit is to deny sin (see vv. 8, 10).

Let me illustrate this by looking at the word *faith*. We are saved by faith, according to Ephesians 2:8, 9 and a host of other New Testament verses. After someone is saved, can he or she ever quit believing? Of course not. If faith is real, it will certainly continue. Belief is not a one-time thing. For example, 1 John 5:1 says, "Whoever believes that Jesus is the Christ is born of God." Literally, that could be translated, "Whoever is believing . . . is born of God." That is what Jesus implied when He said, "If you continue in My word, then you are truly disciples of Mine" (John 8:31). And again, "Who is the one who overcomes the world, but he who [is believing] that Jesus is the Son of God?" (1 John 5:5). So faith that is real will last forever.

If the confession of sin that leads to salvation is real, the sinner will go on agreeing with God about his sin as well. What brings us to Jesus Christ—acknowledging our sin and believing in Him—continues through our whole Christian life. That is what the Spirit of God is saying. Those who are saved will continue to believe, and they will continue to confess. Perhaps I can sum it up in four important words: *Continual confession characterizes Christians.*

There may be varying degrees of confession. Some may confess more frequently than others. Some seem more sensitive to their sin than others. Perhaps there are even differing degrees of repentance.

Some Christians seem to know a repentance that is fuller or deeper than that of others. Certainly the same thing is true of faith, isn't it? Some have more faith than others. Jesus said that even faith as small as a grain of mustard seed is enough (Matthew 17:20). Still, confession and faith must be present in some measure, and as one grows in the Christian life, he will find himself confessing more and believing with stronger faith than when he first believed.

We must be honest in this area. The blessing of God is reserved for a confessing heart. If we have a superficial relationship with God, our confession will be superficial: "O Lord, I sinned again today, and You know it. There are a whole lot of things I've done wrong, and I don't have time to go into them. Amen." You've probably heard people say, "Well, sure, I'm a sinner, but isn't everyone?" If that's your attitude toward sin, I feel constrained to urge you to examine yourself to see if you're truly a believer (see 2 Corinthians 13:5).

Don't just tacitly admit that you are a sinner; agree with God concerning your sin. If you could see the depths of your sin from the bottom of your heart—just once, the way God sees it—your life would never be the same again.

CAN A CHRISTIAN BE OUT OF FELLOWSHIP WITH GOD?

Some people say that confession is important because it restores fellowship with God, which they believe is broken by sin. We sin, fellowship is broken; we confess, fellowship is restored. But that is not what Scripture teaches. Our fellowship with God never changes, regardless of how we fail. Genuine fellowship cannot be broken by sin and therefore cannot be restored by confession. We have been led astray by the usual understanding of the word *fellowship*. We use it to mean "friendship, intimacy, relationship between persons." But the Greek word is *koinonia*, meaning "partnership." Our partnership with God can never be broken by sin, Satan, or anything else in the universe (see Romans 8:32-39). Something does happen when we sin, but it is not broken fellowship. It is forfeiture of joy. "These things we write unto you, that your joy may be full" (1 John 1:4, KJV). Although our fellowship cannot be broken, we can foul up our lives so that we lose our joy. Many, many Christians have done that very thing.

I don't deny that in sinning, a believer loses a certain intimacy, a warmhearted experience, a sense of nearness to God. Something does go away, but Scripture speaks of it as lost joy rather than lost fellowship.

What is the fastest way to regain the joy of your salvation? Do what David did—confess. He prayed, "Restore to me the joy of Your salvation" (Psalm 51:12). God then returns His joy to you.

WINNING THE BATTLES

So far we have seen that *cleansing* and *confession* characterize the Christian life. A third quality common to every believer is *conquering*. God liberates the Christian. That is, for the first time He gives the believer an ability to do what is right. That is something we never could do before we were saved. We were dead in our trespasses and sins, slaves to sin. We had no choice but to sin. Now we have strength to prevail over sin.

Who needs it? a Christian may say to himself, or even aloud. *Since I'm going to be a sinner for the rest of my life and I have to keep confessing, there's no need to strive for holiness—especially since I'm cleansed anyway. I'll just live as I please.*

John responds to that philosophy, "My little children [he was ninety years old when he wrote this, so he could use that expression], I am writing these things to you that you may not sin" (1 John 2:1). I like that! You will never hear a simpler exhortation than that: "Don't sin!"

Perhaps you're wondering, *Why did John say that? If I'm always going to be confessing and always going to be cleansed, isn't it ridiculous to say, "Don't sin"?*

No, it isn't ridiculous, because we do not *have* to sin. That sounds like a contradiction, but it isn't. Within every believer lies the power for victory over sin. That is why I use the word *conquering*. We can conquer sin. "Sin shall not be master over you, for you are not under law but under grace" (Romans 6:14). Sin has no more power over those of us who are in Christ. Romans 8:13 says we can mortify sin, or put it to death. Unbelievers cannot win over sin, but Christians certainly can.

One indisputable mark of spiritual maturity is the decreasing frequency of sin. Why would God tell us not to sin if we didn't have a choice in the matter? Paul said the same thing: "Become sober-minded as you ought, and stop sinning" (1 Corinthians 15:34). "Be angry, and yet do not sin" (Ephesians 4:26). "For the grace of God has appeared, bringing salvation to all men, instructing us to deny ungodliness and worldly desires and to live sensibly, righteously and godly in the present age" (Titus 2:11, 12). In other words, we are not to sin. I once preached a sermon entitled "Four Things the Holy Spirit Does for You, Whether You Like It or Not." Among those sovereign works of the Spirit is subduing the flesh. You cannot conquer in your flesh, but the Holy Spirit working in you can.

JESUS, OUR ADVOCATE

Let's conclude this section on sin and confession with John's brief summary: "If anyone sins, we have an Advocate with the Father, Jesus Christ the righteous; and He Himself is the propitiation for our sins; and not for ours only, but also for those of the whole world" (1 John 2:1, 2). John says, in effect, if we do sin, we have Someone to cover for us. Again, he is not speaking of a habitual disobedience or sin as a course of life, but of individual sinful acts that interrupt our walk of faith. When we do commit such an act, it is cleansed.

What is an advocate? It is the same word translated "Helper" in John 15:26. It means a lawyer for the defense—someone called alongside to help. Whenever we sin, do you think God accuses us? No, but Satan does. "Look at him, God. That child of Yours sinned." The devil is like a prosecuting attorney.

But our Advocate, the Lord Jesus Christ, rises and says, "It is taken care of, Father. I bore it in My body. I paid the penalty." The Righteous One who has saved us from all unrighteousness, the One who is holy and has made the perfect sacrifice, personally defends us. So Satan is foiled. "Who will bring a charge against God's elect?" asks Romans 8:33.

There you have it. As those redeemed by our Lord Jesus Christ, we are cleansed. As cleansed ones, we confess our sins. And as those who confess, we conquer. No matter how deep your guilt, no matter how frequent your failure, come to God in contrite confession and let Him do His work in your life.

One of the most thrilling scenes in English literature comes at the conclusion of *Mutiny on the Bounty*. Some seamen are being court-martialed before the Royal Navy. These men are on trial for mutiny, facing the possibility of death by hanging. Roger Byam, a young sailor, is one of those on trial. Because he is a person of loyalty and integrity, Byam is granted a pardon by the king. Though judged guilty, he is acquitted and restored to rank, and the record of his crime is forever expunged.

That is what David asked for—and received. And that is what every believer receives in Christ. We believe God is a forgiving God, and in response and thanks, we confess our sin to Him, turning from it, lest we stamp on His grace.

7

LOVE

Unlocking the Bridal Suite

At the time of Moses, God gave His people the Ten Commandments. But by the time of the Lord Jesus' walk on earth, the legal traditions of the rabbis totaled in the thousands. There is no way any person can keep thousands of laws perfectly. So the Jewish leaders made an accommodation. They divided all their rules and regulations into heavy laws and light laws. "The heavy laws are just that," they said. "They're binding. The light laws? Well, you can give a little on those."

Some rabbis even went further and taught that if a man selected just one great precept to observe, he could disregard all the others.

Against this background, a lawyer came to Jesus with a question: "Teacher, which is the great commandment in the Law?" (Matthew 22:36). Jesus replied, "'You shall love the Lord your God with all your heart, and with all your soul, and with all your mind.' This is the great and foremost commandment. The second is like it, 'You shall love your neighbor as yourself.' On these two commandments depend the whole Law and the Prophets" (vv. 37-40).

Thus our Lord established love as the highest of all spiritual virtues. The apostle Paul confirmed the superiority of love: "Now faith, hope, love, abide these three; but the greatest of these is love" (1 Corinthians 13:13).

THE EXAMPLE OF PETER

What is involved in keeping this first commandment that our Lord termed the greatest? I know of no better illustration than that furnished by one of the twelve disciples in John 21:2-17.

"I'm going fishing!" Peter said one day after the death and resurrection of the Lord Jesus Christ. He was saying to the other disciples that he was going back to the fishing business, returning to what he used to do. Since Peter was the leader, the rest of the fellows said, "We're going too," and they all followed Peter dutifully to the boat. The Lord then rerouted all the fish in the Sea of Galilee so that none went near the boat. So Peter and the others labored all night with nothing to show for it.

"Have you caught anything?" a stranger called to them at dawn on the next day.

"No," they answered.

"Cast the net on the other side of the boat, and you'll catch some fish." Who knows why the disciples obeyed such an unusual suggestion. Perhaps it was the innate authority in the stranger's voice. But they did as He suggested. Meanwhile, the Lord supernaturally directed the fish to the right side of the boat. The catch was so big that the disciples couldn't even get their nets aboard the boat.

"It is the Lord," John said. Hearing that, Peter threw himself into the water and swam ashore.

Jesus invited them to breakfast—a meal He had prepared, perhaps supernaturally. As Peter and the others sat there, eating with the Lord of Glory, Peter must have thought, *What a clod I am! What a disobedient, inadequate person! I've failed again.* Peter had failed virtually every test the Lord had given him. He just couldn't succeed. There must have been tears in his eyes and grief and pain in his heart as he looked at Jesus, whom he loved so much but had served so poorly.

At last the Lord spoke. "Peter, do you love Me more than these?"

These what? Well, maybe these things—the boat, the fish, the nets, the sea, or the whole fishing business. Or perhaps the Lord was asking if Peter loved Him more than the other disciples did.

Peter had claimed on one occasion that he was more faithful than the others. Undoubtedly he had believed his love for the Master was greater than theirs.

"Peter, do you love Me? Do you genuinely love Me?" The Lord used the word *agapao*, meaning the highest kind of supreme love.

How long Peter took in replying, we do not know. But he said, "Yes, Lord, You know that I love You." But Peter used a different word—*phileo*—denoting respect and devotion. It was as if he replied, "I like You a lot."

Perhaps Peter felt his love was supreme, but shamed by his recent failure, he could not stand before the Lord and claim that kind of love. Remember, he had denied the Lord three times on the night of the crucifixion, and Jesus had looked him in the eyes when the cock crowed. It would have been ridiculous for him to say, "Lord, I supremely love You, but I don't stand with You when it might cost me something."

I once asked a five-year-old how he could show his parents that he loved them. "I could obey them," he replied. Even he understood that love is best displayed in that way.

It is not right to claim supreme love if you do not obey the one you claim to love. So Peter did not make that claim. Since Peter had denied the Lord on three occasions, Christ gave him three opportunities to redeem himself. Jesus said to him a second time, "Simon, son of Jonas [the Lord called him by his old name because he was acting like his old self], do you love Me?" Again, the Lord used the word *agapao*.

"Yes, Lord, You know I like You a lot."

Jesus probed a third time, but now he adopted Peter's word for love. "Simon, do you even like Me a lot?" The Bible says Peter was grieved. Why? Because of being queried three times? No. Because the Lord was challenging Peter's testimony, questioning the level of Peter's love.

"Lord, You know all things. You know that I like You." Peter was implying, "Don't just hear what I say. Look at my heart."

When I was a little boy, I used to think about the doctrine of omniscience—the fact that God knows everything about everything—a terrible problem if we're not obeying Him. My dad used to warn me, "We may not know, but God knows! He sees what you do, Johnny." I wondered why God would waste His day just watching what I did.

As I matured in my understanding and grew up, I came to realize that in many ways I'm like Peter. There are some days when the only way God would ever know that I loved Him was by His omniscience. I realized this doctrine had a positive side. Aren't you glad that on the days when your life does not make your testimony very clear you can say, "Lord, I'm sorry about the way I act. Would You read my heart and know that I love You?" That's what Peter did.

THE CHARACTERISTICS OF OUR LOVE FOR GOD

What kind of love did Jesus seek from Peter—and what does He seek from us? Is it an emotional love—a sentimental kind of thing? Are we supposed to feel spiritual goose bumps toward the Lord? Well, there are times in my life when I don't have this overwhelming feeling of warmth and intimacy toward Christ. And I can't just whip up an emotional reaction. But that is not what the Lord is talking about. We learn what real love is as we look further at this incident between Peter and Jesus.

Sacrifice

In John 21:18, 19, our Lord warned Peter about what it would cost to follow Him:

> *"Truly, truly, I say to you, when you were younger, you used to gird yourself and walk wherever you wished; but when you grow old, you will stretch out your hands and someone else will gird you, and bring you where you do not wish to go." Now this He said, signifying by what kind of death he would glorify God.*

The phrase "stretch out your hands" speaks of crucifixion. "Peter, you're going to be crucified. Peter, do you really love Me? Then die for Me."

That is what it means to love God with all your heart, soul, and mind. This kind of love is willing to make a sacrifice of itself. It is not the sentimental kind of love we hear so much about. It isn't simply a feeling. Peter had that already, but it wasn't enough. So now Jesus offered Peter a way to exhibit his love. He didn't just say, "Peter, does it feel nice inside to love Me? Do you feel slightly warm between your fourth and fifth ribs?" No, He asked for sacrifice.

How can you tell if you love the Lord Jesus Christ? It hinges on whether you are willing to sacrifice in order to do His will daily. In the first century, the ultimate sacrifice could very well mean physical death. The Roman general Varus reportedly put down an insurrection in Galilee by lining the road with crosses. Peter had witnessed that kind of death; it was fresh in his mind from the Lord's crucifixion. He knew what such a sacrifice would mean.

Peter had always sworn that he could handle dying for Jesus, but he had recently failed miserably under intense pressure. Perhaps he was doubting his own fortitude. Yet here was the Lord making a flat prophecy that in the end Peter was going to be faithful. I think Peter must have said to himself, *Wonderful! At last I'll make it! I'll stand true to the Lord. I won't fizzle out at the end.*

Obedience

A second quality of the love our Lord demands is obedience. Not only is it self-sacrificial, but it is submissive. "Follow Me!" the Lord commanded Peter (John 21:19). When Jesus got up and walked away, Peter arose and followed, literally interpreting His command. Yes, it is true that Peter digressed for a moment by turning, seeing John, and asking the Lord what lay ahead for the beloved disciple. "That's none of your business, Peter," the Lord said in effect. And again He commanded, "Follow Me" (vv. 20-22). And Peter did—for the rest of his life.

What is involved in giving sacrificial obedience to the Lord out of our love for Him? In my life it involves a number of things—one of which is spending five to six hours a day in my study, poring over the Word of God. Quite frankly, however, on some days when I enter the office, I am tired and don't feel like studying. I would like to do something else, like dusting off the golf clubs and playing eighteen holes. But instead I grit my teeth and struggle through a day of intense study. At the end of that day, the only emotion I feel is the sense of accomplishment of having done it. But in working, I have loved the Lord Jesus Christ over against myself. I have fulfilled His will and sacrificed in order to do it.

Now that may be a small thing, but it demonstrates the principle of sacrificial obedience. Such obedience done out of love is not an emotional thing, but a fulfilling of 1 John 2:5: "Whoever keeps His word, in him the love of God has truly been perfected. By this we know that we are in Him." The love that God seeks—love of heart, mind, and soul—obeys.

THE CHARACTERISTICS OF OUR LOVE FOR OTHERS

Now let's go back to our Lord's reply to the lawyer who asked about the greatest commandment. First, we are to love God; second, we are to love others. Scripture elaborates repeatedly on this point. For example, 1 Thessalonians says we have been taught by God to love one another. In view of that, we are to *increase* in love toward one another (4:9, 10). And Peter writes that we are to love one another with a pure heart, "fervently" (1 Peter 1:22). The word "fervently" comes from a Greek term meaning "extended or stretched out." We are to reach out as far as necessary to love others.

Just as love for God is not an emotionally induced feeling, neither is loving others. This kind of love also demands sacrifice. Writing about it in 1 John 3:14, 15, the apostle John switched from a statement about loving the brethren—plural—to loving a brother—singular. Some people say, "Well, I love the brethren collectively—I just can't stand some individuals."

A well-known *Peanuts* cartoon shows Lucy accusing her little brother, Linus, of not loving his fellowman. "I love mankind," was his indignant response. "It's people I can't stand!" It is very easy to love the whole wide world, and it is easy to love the church. However, it may be very difficult to love one particular person. But the love our Lord calls for is a practical, personal kind of love that is expressed primarily to individuals.

Love in Action

When I first came to Grace Community Church, I wanted badly to love everyone, but I couldn't figure out how to get the emotional feeling I thought was necessary. Some people were kind of irritating, and some even purposely made things difficult for me. I wanted to love them, but I didn't know how. One day I went to a man who was particularly difficult, put my arm around him, and said, "I want you to know something. If there's any way I can ever serve you, I'd sure love to have the opportunity." The opportunity came. My attitude toward him didn't change because of how I felt about him emotionally, but because I learned to love him by serving him.

Loving others is not a question of patting someone on the back and saying, "You're so wonderful, so irresistible. I love you!" We show love by making personal sacrifices to meet someone's need. Sometimes I'm asked how I can minister to individuals in a large church. It is not by running around to everyone and expressing love, but by making sacrifices in my life to help them to grow spiritually. I care enough about them to do what is necessary in my life to bring them into conformity to Jesus Christ.

How do we best know that God loves us? Has He ever shouted it from heaven or written it in the sky? No; we perceive the love of God because Christ laid down His life for us. God put His Son on a cross on our behalf. That is how He expressed His love—through sacrifice. Since Christ "laid down His life for us . . . we ought to lay down our lives for the brethren" (1 John 3:16). Death isn't always the price; sometimes love requires the sacrifice of our possessions or our time or whatever. "But whoever has the world's goods, and beholds his brother in need and closes his heart against him, how does the love of God abide in him?" (1 John 3:17). If we see someone who has a need, we must meet that need as far as we're able, or we prove ourselves to be deficient in love.

"Well," someone interjects, "before we can love someone, we have to love ourselves. After all, the Bible says in James 2:8 we are to love our neighbors as we love ourselves." That is a popular concept. But it is not what James 2:8 teaches. Psychologists have made a business out of misinterpreting that verse. They say you must have the proper self-image, and if you do not have an exalted impression of yourself and all that, you will never be able to love other people correctly. That's a serious misunderstanding. It stems from the notion that love is sentimental. When the Bible speaks of love, it describes something quite different.

What does it mean to love others as we love ourselves? Look at James 2:1: "My brethren, do not hold your faith in our glorious Lord Jesus Christ with an attitude of personal favoritism." The text goes on to give the illustration of a rich man and a poor man visiting a congregation and being treated differently. James is saying that as Christians we are not to treat certain people with respect while we treat others with indifference. Rather, to fulfill the royal law, we are to treat everyone as we would treat ourselves. That means that whatever great sacrifices we make for our own comfort, we should make for the comfort of others, without respect to their status in life. It has nothing to do with our psychological self, but it has to do with our service toward others.

Just stop, for example, and consider the lengths we go to make ourselves comfortable. That is the same way we should meet the needs of others. The way we treat our own desires, we should treat the desires of others. We should love them in terms of self-sacrificing service, just as we make sacrifices for our own benefit. Are you willing to do that? Are you willing to give up whatever it is that makes you comfortable in order to provide for the comfort of someone else? Are you willing to sacrifice the things you enjoy so that another's need may be met? That is loving your neighbor as yourself. It is not psychological; it is sacrificial.

Love in Humility

Perhaps the best example of self-sacrificing love for others was given by our Lord Himself. On the night before He suffered and died, the Lord did not tell His disciples in the upper room, "I love you. I'd like to give you a discussion of divine love and tell you how it works."

Instead, as we saw in the previous chapter, our Lord washed His disciples' feet. John 13:3-5 tells us:

> *Jesus, knowing that the Father had given all things into His hands, and that He had come forth from God and was going back to God, rose from supper, and laid aside His garments; and taking a towel, He girded Himself. Then He poured water into the basin, and began to wash the disciples' feet and to wipe them with the towel with which He was girded.*

God in the flesh was stooping to wash dirt off the feet of His weak, sinning disciples. Now that's love!

It is precisely the kind of love the Lord demands of His disciples. Following His amazing example of self-humiliation, Jesus said, "A new commandment I give to you, that you love one another, even as I have loved you, that you also love one another. By this all men will know that you are My disciples, if you have love for one another" (vv. 34, 35).

How had Jesus demonstrated His love for them? By washing their dirty feet, by taking the role of a slave, by doing the distasteful thing, the sacrificial thing. Loving one another is not just feeling little pangs of emotion. It is serving. When we willingly sacrifice what we want for the good of another, when we choose to fill the need of someone instead of satisfying our own need, then we really love (no matter what our emotions may be). That is what God expects.

The apostle John sums up love as a key to spiritual growth in simple and familiar words: "Little children, let us not love with word or with tongue, but in deed and truth" (1 John 3:18).

8

PRAYER

Unlocking the Inner Sanctum

What could be richer or more rewarding than the Christian faith? We who are in Christ have all spiritual blessings (Ephesians 1:3). We were chosen by God before the foundation of the world (1:4). We have complete forgiveness (1:7). We have an inheritance beyond anything we could imagine (1:14). We have complete security (1:14). We are alive with new life (2:5). We are the objects of eternal grace (2:7). We are God's masterpiece (2:10). We are in union with Christ (2:13). We are members of one body (2:16) with access to God by one Spirit (2:18). We are the temple of God (2:21) and the dwelling place of the Spirit (2:22). And we are powerful (3:20).

What extraordinary statements! How great is the Christian life when seen in the light of who we are in Christ! Moreover, we do not have to earn this exalted position. It is already ours through our salvation in the Lord Jesus Christ.

The final three chapters of Ephesians go beyond the positional aspects of our life and get into practical issues. For example, we are commanded to walk intelligently as believers (4:17), to walk in God's love (5:2), and to walk in the light (5:8). The apostle Paul spells out in great detail how we can do those things.

This presentation of our sufficiency in Christ has no rival in all the Word of God. If any believer studies Ephesians carefully and concludes that he lacks some spiritual resource, he is blind. We do not need more of the Holy Spirit, more love, more grace, or more anything else. In Christ we have it all. We have everything we need to grow and mature.[1]

THE DANGER OF OVERCONFIDENCE

At this point, however, a potentially destructive problem arises. I call it spiritual overconfidence or doctrinal egotism. It is a latent danger in the Christian life that believers who have a very deep knowledge of doctrine and a fairly effective grip on practical spiritual principles become self-satisfied. Then heartrending, passionate, constant prayer finds no place in their lives. I have seen this condition develop time and again. As we gain knowledge, a creeping self-dependence can evolve that eliminates the vitality of a real prayer life.

To guard against this danger, Paul commands believers to "pray without ceasing" (1 Thessalonians 5:17). He summons us to a life of prayer. Regardless of how much we have in Christ, we must pray. Prayer is an essential key to spiritual growth.

For an analogy on the necessity of prayer, think of the atmosphere and breathing. The atmosphere exerts pressure on your lungs and forces you to take it in. You breathe very naturally in response to this pressure, instead of consciously going around working to inhale air. In fact, it is much more difficult to hold your breath than it is to breathe. You would never say, "Oh, I'm so tired today from all the effort I've used breathing." But you would be very tired if you had been fighting not to breathe—fighting against the natural processes that enable you to breathe almost effortlessly.

The same is true in prayer. Prayer is the natural thing for a Christian. It is the Christian's vital breath. The reason some Christians feel so fatigued and defeated is that they are holding their breath spiritually when they should be opening their hearts to God to accept the atmosphere all about them—His divine presence. The one who is not faithful in prayer constantly struggles against his own spiritual nature. He is holding his spiritual breath. And that is spiritually debilitating.

Why would any Christian not pray, since prayer is like breathing? Good question. The answer is sin. Sin in our lives stifles prayer.

When we are not willing to confess and to forsake it, we really do not want to pray, because prayer opens us up to God's presence, and we do not feel comfortable there.

Another reason for prayerlessness is selfishness. Of course, that's also a form of sin. Selfishness is surely the primary reason people do not pray. It manifests itself in symptomatic sins such as laziness or unconcern or indifference. Look into your life, and you can probably identify some sin that keeps you from prayer. And if you are not praying, you are suffocating. That is deadly!

A GUIDE TO PROPER PRAYER

In the last two chapters of Ephesians, Paul gives two brief but pointed emphases on prayer. Each has a great lesson to teach.

The first emphasis, a general instruction, is found in Ephesians 6:18: "With all prayer and petition pray at all times in the Spirit, and with this in view, be on the alert with all perseverance and petition for all the saints." Paul repeats the word "all" four times in that verse. Taken together, these make up four different points regarding prayer. We might label them the "alls" of prayer.

The Variety of Prayer

The first "all" speaks of the types of prayer: "With all prayer and petition." "Prayer" here is a general word pertaining to its many forms and character. For example, you can pray publicly or privately, verbally or silently. You can pray those deliberately planned prayers you find in a prayer book, or you can pray those spontaneous prayers that just flow out of your heart. You can request something from God, or you can give Him thanks for what He has given. You can be kneeling, standing, sitting, lying down, or even driving. There are many ways to pray because God has designed prayer to go along with every kind of emotion and every kind of experience. We have a variety of forms of prayer to fit every situation and circumstance.

The second word Paul uses describes a particular type of prayer—"petition" (KJV, "supplication"). That is best defined as a specific request. How often we generalize, "God, bless the missionaries. God, bless the church." Those are not specifics; they are generalities. Such vague requests are likely to lead to unclear answers—if any at all.

My daughter had a habit of generalizing. One night at the end of a long, tired day, she knelt by her bed and prayed, "God, bless everything in the world. Amen." I had to tell her that this was not a very good prayer. I conducted a little theological discussion to try to impress on her that God wanted her to ask Him for specific things that were on her heart, not "everything in the world." Supplication must be specific.

The Frequency of Prayer

The second "all" indicates the frequency of prayer: "pray at all times." When should we pray? Someone says, "I think it's in the morning." Another insists, "I like to do it at night." Really? When do you breathe? Would you say, "Oh, I take a few gasps of air in the morning" or "I get my air at night"? How ridiculous! We must be praying always and always praying. The Greek construction speaks of praying on every occasion.

I think Paul really meant this! And when our Lord Jesus said we ought to pray at all times (Luke 18:1), I think He meant it too. If our Savior Himself felt a tremendous desire and need to pray, knowing that He was God in the flesh (John 17), how much more strongly do we need to pray, even though we know our position in Christ?

The frequency of our prayers was a common theme in the apostle Paul's writings. "Be anxious for nothing, but in everything by prayer and supplication with thanksgiving let your requests be made known to God" (Philippians 4:6). "Devote yourselves to prayer" (Colossians 4:2). "Pray without ceasing" (1 Thessalonians 5:17). Paul not only talked about the importance of prayer—he lived it. Paul was constantly praying for someone.

How is it possible to be always praying? First, we have to define our terms. To "pray at all times" means that we are God-conscious—that we see everything that happens with reference to

God. That is, we live in constant awareness of His presence. Let me illustrate. You get up in the morning and look out on a beautiful day with a beautiful sky. What is your first thought? Perhaps it is, *Thank You, Lord, for this great day You have made.* That is praying at all times. Then you go outside and see your neighbor who is living in sin. So you pray, *God, save my neighbor!* You get into your car and drive down a street and see signs advertising topless bars. You think, *God, what is this world coming to? God, help me reach those people who are lost and sick.* Once again you are praying at all times.

Praying constantly is not just reciting some formula prayer thirty-five times. It has nothing to do with prayer beads, repetitious prayers, or any kind of structured, ritual praying. Praying without ceasing means seeing things from God's viewpoint. When we see a hurt, we ask God to heal it; when we notice a problem, we turn to God for a solution. Unceasing prayer means seeing a Christian brother who has a need and praying for him, or seeing a man in trouble and asking God to deliver him. It is communing with God about what you know dishonors Him. All these exemplify what it means to pray without stopping. At every waking moment we are praising God for something wonderful or interceding for someone—living in unbroken communion with Him.

The Attitudes of Prayer

Next in Ephesians 6:18, Paul considered the proper attitudes of prayer: "Be on the alert with all perseverance and petition." "Perseverance" means "endurance"—sticking to the task. When you pray for something, stay with it until you have an answer—like the man in Luke 11:5-8 who kept banging away at the door until his neighbor opened up to give him bread for his unexpected guests. God says in effect that He will respond in a similar manner. He listens for constant, persevering prayer.

If we are to persevere in prayer, it is important to "be on the alert." We cannot pray intelligently unless we are alert to what is going on. Many Christians forget or ignore Peter's plea to "be of sound judgment and sober spirit for the purpose of prayer" (1 Peter

4:7). He urged us to maintain sleepless, incessant, persevering, and vigilant prayer.

Do you know what is going on in your home? What about your wife? Do you pray for her faithfully, without ceasing? Do you pray for her constantly, asking God to make her the kind of woman she ought to be? Do you faithfully pray that God will bless her and enrich her life and bring her to spiritual maturity?

What about your husband? Do you pray that he might be God's man in every sense of the word? Do you pray that he might be like Christ as he gives spiritual direction to your home? Do you petition God that your husband might make the right decisions? Do you pray that God will help him in his work? Do you become aware of the problems and conflicts he faces and then pray about them?

What about your children? Do you pray that God will build them up in the Spirit, that they will be strong in the Lord, that He will keep them from the evil one?

What about your neighbors? The people around you? The kids at school? The sick? Others who need your prayers? When someone shares a need, do you really pray or do you merely say, "We'll be praying for you" and then forget?

We used to have a man in our church who had in his bookcase a whole stack of notebooks of all the requests that he had prayed for and that God had answered through the years. When I learned what he was doing, he was working on his fifteenth or sixteenth notebook. This fellow was "alert"! When he heard of someone who had a need, he would write it down and pray—a great practice to follow. Then he would record when the answer was received. His notebooks were a visible testimony to the faithfulness of a God who answers prayer.

On one occasion someone told me, "MacArthur, I'm going to put you on my prayer list for six months." My first reaction was, *Is that all I get?* But my second reaction was to praise the Lord. It is unusual to have someone commit himself to pray for you for a certain period of time. I would rather have someone pray faithfully for me for six months than have someone pray sporadically for me for a longer period of time.

The Objects of Prayer

The fourth "all" that Paul speaks about concerns the objects of prayer. The direct object of our prayers, of course, is God. This suggests a very important principle that is stated clearly in John 14:13, 14: "Whatever you ask in My name, that will I do, that the Father may be glorified in the Son. If you ask Me anything in My name, I will do it."

Here Jesus comforted His disciples in their sorrow over His leaving. They were thinking how bad it would be without Jesus present to fill their needs, hear their cries, answer their requests, and protect them. After all, He had given them food, helped them catch fish, provided tax money, loved them, taught them, and provided a shoulder for them to cry on. How could they survive without Him? This promise that Jesus gave filled that void. Even though Jesus was going to leave them, they would still have total access to all His supply for them. Prayer would remove the distance. What a promise!

However, a condition determines the Lord's response to prayer—prayer must be "in My name." As we saw in chapter 3, praying in Jesus' name is not simply tacking a phrase onto the end of our prayers. Perhaps this subject is worth another look now, since we're considering the question of how to pray.

First, praying in Jesus' name means standing in His place, fully identifying with Him, asking God for intervention by virtue of our union with His Son. Thus, when we truly ask in Jesus' name, it is as if He were the petitioner.

Second, it means that we plead before God the merits of His blessed Son. We ask that an answer to our prayer be granted on Christ's behalf. We desire something for His sake. When we truly ask in Jesus' name, He becomes the receiver.

Third, as we have seen, praying in Jesus' name means we pray only for that which is consistent with His perfection—something for His glory.

To pray in Jesus' name, then, is to seek what He seeks, to promote what He desires, to give Him glory. We can only rightly ask God for that which will glorify the Son.

So end your prayers with something like, "Father, this I ask because I know this is what Jesus would want for His own glory." Affirm that in your heart at the end of each prayer, and you will eliminate all selfish requests. We pray in Jesus' name; to Him and for Him we pray. What could be more practical than that? If people understood that simple principle better, they would eliminate a lot of unnecessary and extraneous praying.

Paul also mentions the indirect object of our prayers—"all the saints." What compels us to pray for each other? For one thing, as members of the body of Christ we are all engaged in a common battle. "For our struggle is not against flesh and blood, but against the rulers, against the powers, against the world forces of this darkness, against the spiritual forces of wickedness in the heavenly places" (Ephesians 6:12). We struggle to win victory through the name of Christ and to exalt Him by our lives. Since that is true, we have to expand our horizons above our own individual struggles and think in terms of the whole body of Christ. We are to be concerned not only for our own ultimate triumph, but for the spiritual victory of all other believers.

Often we believers think of ourselves as separate entities. So many times we get the idea that we exist independent of everyone else. Of course we don't. Just as the human body cannot move forward unless all the members move, neither can the body of Christ.

Second, just as the body of Christ ministers through spiritual gifts, so we also minister through prayer. Are spiritual gifts for selfish purposes? Does God want me to exercise my gift for my benefit? Should I take my spiritual gift and go off to a cabin somewhere and teach myself? Should I stand in front of a mirror and preach? That is laughable. My spiritual gift is to be exercised for others' benefit. So the prayer life and prayer power that I have is not for me either—it is for others. I am supposed to pray for them, and they in turn should pray for me.

God designed it that way for our unity. When one part of the physical body is hurt or sick, all the other parts come to its aid. If my eye is injured, my eyelid directly protects it; but indirectly the rest of my body also functions to send healing to my eye. My reflexes go on alert to keep anything from touching the wounded member. Similarly, if a brother has a need, we may minister to him directly through the exercise of our spiritual gifts or we may minister indirectly by praying.

I'm certain we would see great things happen in the church if we really prayed for each other. Even though we enjoy an exalted position in relation to Christ, we still have a desperate need for the prayers of other believers. Likewise we need to be constantly asking God to work in specific ways for specific saints.

How do we get to know one another's needs? That is a problem. Often people are reluctant to share their burdens. So we must take the initiative and open up a little and get to the place where we ourselves are willing to share. Someone else may have the same problem we do! We can pray for each other. Face it—no one can possibly bear our burden if he does not know what it is.

That does not mean we have to tell everything to everyone That would be poor judgment. But let us at least start sharing our needs with those we know we can trust and start praying for one another. That will take us out of spectator Christianity and get us into the arena where the struggle goes on. We need to remember that all of us are at war spiritually. If we really believe in the power of prayer, we will fervently pray and see God do things that He otherwise wouldn't.

A SAMPLE PRAYER LIST

Paul closes his comments about prayer with his second emphasis—a specific application. That fits in with his usual pattern of first teaching, then giving a practical correlation. In this context, Paul follows the "alls" set forth in Ephesians 6:18 with a precise command in verses 19, 20: "Pray on my behalf, that utterance may be given to me in the opening of my mouth, to make known with boldness the mystery of the gospel, for which I am an ambassador in chains; that in proclaiming it I may speak boldly, as I ought to speak."

What a man, this Paul! He laid down the principle and then said, "I'm the fellow you can start with!" Note further that Paul didn't ask for his physical needs, as many today might have done. As great as his physical and emotional needs were, he requested prayer that he might possess the message of God and then have the courage to give it out. So the apostle was not asking for prayer selfishly; he asked that his ministry might continue unimpeded, even if he was in jail at the time. He uses himself as a living illustration, sharing his life with his readers in order that they might pray for him.

That sets a pattern of prayer for us. We are to be primarily concerned with the spiritual dimension. This means that instead of praying only for someone to be delivered from physical ills or trials, we should be praying that he would be in a right relationship with God so he can relate to the trial with the proper attitude. Do not be so shortsighted that you stop praying for physical needs, but principally it is people's *spiritual* welfare that God is concerned with. Our trials are designed to bring spiritual growth. So don't just pray for an end to the trials; pray for the growth that God desires. Paul's prayers were always in line with spiritual objectives; physical ones were never the issue.

As you learn to pray as Paul instructs, you will find yourself becoming God-conscious and selfless. And as you humble yourself, spend time with the Holy Spirit, and pray under His supervision, you will find your life being molded into the very image of Jesus Christ. And that's what prayer is all about!

9

HOPE

Unlocking the Hope Chest

Hope is one of the greatest words of the Christian vocabulary. In 1 Corinthians 13:13, Paul gave a triad of Christian virtues, and one of them is hope. Strong hope is a crucial aspect of spiritual maturity.

The very word itself shines like light in darkness, joy in sorrow, life in death.

Sadly, however, many cling to false hopes. They erroneously count on something worthless for security, usually their own good works or a misunderstanding of God's benevolence. Others maintain a vain hope in gold or silver. Some of them may be counting on heaven, anticipating a happy afterlife; but without Jesus their hope is groundless. The Scriptures say, "For what is the hope of the godless . . . when God requires his life?" (Job 27:8).

In other words, these people have no real hope. Scripture says the entire pagan world is "without hope and without God" (Ephesians 2:12). Look at the heathen philosophies in Paul's day, and you can readily understand why. Some believed that the soul, temporarily imprisoned in the body, would one day reluctantly leave through the last gasp of breath or through an open wound. The soul would then enter hades (or the grave)—the shade world— and would spend eternity bemoaning its existence, without comfort of any kind. The Greek poet Theognis said, "I rejoice in sport in my youth; long enough beneath the earth shall I lie and so be voiceless as a stone, leaving the sunlight which I love. Good man though I am, then shall I see nothing more." That is hopelessness—a hope-lessness without God. Even today we see many people in the world who live without hope, and we can only view them with pity.

Hopelessness is one reason men have devised so many false religions. People must have some kind of expectation for the future if they are to survive the present. Some people delude themselves with false hopes, and others escape through drink or drugs. All that is because life without hope is not worth living.

Romans 8:24 speaks to this issue so far as Christians are con-cerned: "In hope we have been saved, but hope that is seen is not hope; for who hopes for what he already sees?" This verse suggests that many elements of our salvation await some future fulfillment. The fullness of our salvation is a hope for the future.

While we could not begin to investigate all that the Bible says about hope, let us look at some of the general statements. First, the Bible says our hope is to be in God and in God alone. The only secure place for true hope is in Him. In Psalm 43:5 we read, "Why are you in despair, O my soul? And why are you disturbed within me? Hope in God, for I shall again praise Him, the help of my countenance and my God."

The Bible also tells us that hope is a gracious gift from God: "Our Lord Jesus Christ Himself and God our Father . . . has loved us and given us eternal comfort and good hope by grace" (2 Thessalonians 2:16). God grants to man hope, confidence, assur-ance, and security for the future—if we accept His gift.

"Where do I get this gift?" you ask. The Bible says that hope comes through the Scriptures: "For whatever was written in earlier times was written for our instruction, so that through perseverance and the encouragement of the Scriptures we might have hope" (Romans 15:4). When you read, understand, and believe the Word of God, you have hope. If you do not believe the Book, you are hurting for hope. For confidence in the future, trust the Word.

A fourth thing may be said about hope: It is secured by Christ's resurrection. If God were merely to say, "You can trust Me in death; I'll take you through," that would be sufficient. But we have an even stronger hope when we see Christ go through death and come out on the other side. He has conquered death. "Blessed be the God and Father of our Lord Jesus Christ, who according to His great mercy has caused us to be born again to a living hope through the resurrection of Jesus Christ from the dead" (1 Peter 1:3).

Hope is further confirmed in us by the Holy Spirit. "Now may the God of hope fill you with all joy and peace in believing, so that you will abound in hope by the power of the Holy Spirit" (Romans 15:13). One of the ministries of the Holy Spirit is to convince the believer that he has hope for the future.

That knowledge acts as a tremendous defense against Satan as he tries to shake us up about the future. Without hope, we might begin to get shaky. But hope defends us against Satan and his lies. First Thessalonians 5:8 refers to "the hope of salvation" as a "helmet." Satan comes along with his broadsword and wants to split your confidence wide open. But when you remember that the Spirit of God has confirmed to you, by the resurrection of Christ, the gracious gift of God—hope—the sword bounces off your helmet without injuring you.

Let me point out something else about hope. Hope is to be continual. Among the many passages speaking to this is Psalm 71:14: "As for me, I will hope continually, and will praise You yet more and more."

Another wonderful thing about hope is that it produces joy: "How blessed is he whose help is the God of Jacob, whose hope is in the LORD his God" (Psalm 146:5). Why is the psalmist happy? Because hope brings joy.

Furthermore, hope removes the fear of death. When we really hope in God, when we hope in Christ our Savior, there is nothing to fear. Colossians 1:5 refers to "the hope . . . laid up for you in heaven." We know that God has a future for us; we know that He has a promise for us; we know that we have hope for the future because the Lord Jesus lives in us now! Our Lord's resurrection is the basis for this hope, the removal of our fear of death.

Another thing that may be said about hope is that it is secure.

Nothing need ever take away our confidence or steal away our hope. Hebrews 6:17, 18 says that our strong consolation and the hope set before us rest on two immutable things—the fact of God's promise and the fact of God's oath. In other words, our hope is secure because God made the promise and underscored it with an oath.

When will our hope be fulfilled? When Jesus comes: "looking for the blessed hope and the appearing of the glory of our great God and Savior, Christ Jesus" (Titus 2:13). At the return of the Lord—that's when hope will be finally realized.

FIVE ASPECTS OF THE BELIEVER'S HOPE

We could not leave our consideration of this theme without looking at 1 John 2:27—3:3, one of the great passages on hope. We discover in this section five features of the believer's hope.

Our Hope Is Guaranteed by Abiding

When John talks about abiding, he is talking about being saved— about a permanent remaining in Christ, which is the measure of a true believer. That concept goes back to the Lord's words, "If you continue in My word, then you are truly disciples of Mine" (John 8:31). True disciples continue.

What insures that the believer will abide? The Holy Spirit. A paraphrase of 1 John 2:27 might read, "The Holy Spirit has been given to you, and He will abide in you so that you don't need any human teachers. But as the Holy Spirit teaches you all things and is truth and is no lie, even as He has taught you, you shall abide." The Holy Spirit is an internal lie detector. The Holy Spirit is a resident truth teacher. He dwells within every Christian to prevent him or her from ever forsaking the truth.

Now we come to verse 28: "And now, little children, abide in Him." What John is really implying is, "Be real. Be true believers. Be Christians." True Christians will continue in Christ.

We are not absolved of responsibility. Many verses in Scriptures say, in effect, "Here is what God has done for you. Now you go out and do it yourself." (Compare Jude 21 with v. 24; John 17:6 with

2 Timothy 4:7.) Privileges in Scripture never cancel obligations; they only increase them. While our abiding in Christ is insured by the Holy Spirit, we are not released from accountability.

The Spirit is given to us, but that does not exempt us or make us irresponsible. It should not make us indifferent, but rather make us more diligent and more faithful, so that we hold more tightly to those things we know to be true. We are to discipline ourselves to conform to the Spirit's work and His will in our lives. When the Bible says we are to walk in the Spirit, it means to behave ourselves commensurate with the working of the Holy Spirit in our lives.

For example, the Lord said to Peter, "I have prayed for you, that your faith may not fail" (Luke 22:32). A few verses later, the Lord looked the disciples in the eye and said, "Pray that you may not enter into temptation" (v. 40).

In 1 Corinthians 10:13 Paul says, "No temptation has overtaken you but such as is common to man; and God is faithful, who will not allow you to be tempted beyond what you are able, but with the temptation will provide a way of escape also, so that you may be able to endure it." The Corinthians might have said, "Great! God will make a way out of it. God will take care of our problems. God is in control." But then the next verse says, "Flee from idolatry."

The inward working of God's grace never sets aside exhortation. Don't ever accept the sovereign working of God in your life as an excuse for indolence, inactivity, or lack of discipline.

Now let's go back to our text in 1 John and read further: "Now, little children, abide in Him, so that when He appears, we may have confidence and not shrink away from Him in shame at His coming" (2:28). That is a tremendous statement. Not one who is abiding in Christ will be ashamed when Jesus comes back!

The mistakes in our lives will be taken care of through the blood of Christ. The word translated "confidence" literally means "boldness." Jesus is coming, and you can be bold when He gets here. In Revelation 22:12 He says, "Behold, I am coming quickly, and My reward is with Me, to render to every man according to what he has done." Jesus will reward us for our service.

This is thrilling! Let me show you some verses to explain what is called the *bema* or judgment seat of Christ. Paul wrote to his young protégé Timothy:

> For I am already being poured out as a drink offering, and the time of my departure has come. I have fought the good fight, I have finished the course, I have kept the faith; in the future there is laid up for me the crown of righteousness, which the Lord, the righteous Judge, will award to me on that day.
>
> —2 TIMOTHY 4:6-8

What day? The day when Jesus is manifest to his church. Paul adds to verse 8: ". . . and not only to me, but also to all who have loved His appearing." They love it so much, they serve Him. They are believers, they are Christians, they are abiders. And they will be bold in getting their reward.

Second Corinthians 5:10 tells us, "We must all appear before the judgment seat of Christ, so that each one may be recompensed for his deeds in the body, according to what he has done, whether good or bad." The words translated "good or bad" could be better translated "useful or worthless."

To understand that, we have to look at a long parallel passage in 1 Corinthians 3:11-15:

> For no man can lay a foundation other than the one which is laid, which is Jesus Christ. Now if any man builds upon the foundation with gold, silver, precious stones, wood, hay, straw, each man's work will become evident; for the day will show it because it is to be revealed with fire, and the fire itself will test the quality of each man's work. If any man's work which he has built upon it remains, he will receive a reward. If any man's work is burned up, he will suffer loss; but he himself will be saved, yet so as through fire.

"Wood, hay, straw" do not seem to refer to sin. They are, rather, the useless things you do that have little consequence. They are not bad, just useless. All that neutral stuff will go up in smoke.

The only things left will be those attitudes and actions that were totally for Christ. For those you will receive a reward.

Since that is true, we ought to be very slow in judging the works of others. That is not our job; it is His. "Therefore do not go on passing judgment before the time, but wait until the Lord comes who will both bring to light the things hidden in the darkness and disclose the motives of men's hearts; and then each man's praise will come to him from God" (1 Corinthians 4:5). What is every individual at the judgment seat going to have? Praise from God. So when Jesus comes, those of us who abide are going to have confidence when we see Him—confidence because Christ has taken care of our sin, burned up all the stubble, and left only something for which we can be rewarded.

The word translated "confidence" in 1 John 2:28 literally means "outspokenness" or "freedom of speech." It is the same word used in Hebrews 4:16, which invites us to come boldly before the throne of grace. The same word refers to the boldness we have in prayer (1 John 3:21, 22). That same confidence with which we enter the Holy of Holies by the blood of Christ allows us to walk to the judgment seat of Christ without shame because we are abiding in Him.

Of course, when Christ is manifest, there is going to be much shame in people who did not abide in Him, who were not believing. To find out just how ashamed they will be, read Revelation 6:15-17:

> Then the kings of the earth and the great men and the commanders and the rich and the strong and every slave and free man hid themselves in the caves and among the rocks of the mountains; and they said to the mountains and to the rocks, "Fall on us and hide us from the presence of Him who sits on the throne, and from the wrath of the Lamb; for the great day of their wrath has come, and who is able to stand?"

The key to this is found in Mark 8:38. Jesus said, "For whoever is ashamed of Me and My words in this adulterous and sinful generation, the Son of Man will also be ashamed of him when He

comes in the glory of His Father with the holy angels." Who's going
to be ashamed when Jesus comes? The people who were ashamed
of Him and of His words in this age.

True believers—those who abide in Christ—are not going to be
ashamed. In fact, they will be blameless. First Corinthians 1:8 tells us
that we shall be confirmed "to the end, blameless in the day of our
Lord Jesus Christ." Not only that, we are not going to have even a
"spot or wrinkle" to mar our appearance (Ephesians 5:27). Fantastic!

Do you need more proof? Colossians 1:22 says that Christ suffered death "to present you before Him holy and blameless and
beyond reproach." First Thessalonians 3:13 says, "So that He may
establish your hearts without blame in holiness before our God and
Father at the coming of our Lord Jesus." We have a great hope, and
this hope is guaranteed as we abide in Christ. So we have come full
circle back to the apostle John's original point.

Our Hope Is Realized in Righteousness

Hope is made real or visibly genuine by our pattern of life. Look
at the next verse of our text: "If you know that He is righteous,
you know that everyone also who practices righteousness is born
of Him" (1 John 2:29). John uses two different Greek words for
"know" in that verse. The first speaks of knowing something absolutely, the second of knowing by experience. John is saying, "If
you know as an absolute that God is righteous, then you know by
experience that everyone who does righteousness is born of Him."

God is righteous, meaning He is innocent of any evil at all. He
always does right and always makes right judgments. Since children
tend to be like their parents, it is fair to assume that God's children
will be like Him. He is righteous; so you would expect His children
to behave righteously. The people who really have this hope will
not be righteous and blameless only at the *bema*, the judgment seat
of Christ; they will be righteous now because they are born of God.
So if our hope is genuine, it will be realized in a righteous life.

First Peter 1:14 adds something to that: "As obedient children,
do not be conformed to the former lusts which were yours in your
ignorance." He says Christ is coming back (v. 13), and you ought

to be obedient. You should not act as you did before becoming Christians. Peter immediately adds, "But like the Holy One who called you, be holy yourselves in all your behavior; because it is written, 'You shall be holy, for I am holy'" (vv. 15, 16). You can tell a child of God because he acts as a child of God should act. Further, Paul said, "Test yourselves to see if you are in the faith" (2 Corinthians 13:5). How would you examine yourself? You would look at your works, at your fruit. So our hope is realized by a righteous life. True hope will result in holy living.

Our Hope Is Established by Love

First John 3:1 says, "See how great a love the Father has bestowed on us, that we should be called children of God; and such we are. For this reason the world does not know us, because it did not know Him." Love gave us our hope.

I used to wonder, *Couldn't John come up with something better than "see how great a love"? How about super, colossal, stupendous, magnanimous, unbelievable love?* Then I realized that John was simply overwhelmed and astonished. He must have been saying to himself, *I can't believe that God loved me so much that He made me His child. It would be far more than I deserve just to be His slave. It would not have been half bad to be His neighbor and would have been great to be called His friend. But to be His son! I can't get any closer than that!* John couldn't find words to express it. The concept was too great.

The *King James Version* uses the expression "what manner of love." In classical Greek the word translated "what manner" (*potapos*) speaks of a foreign race, country, or tribe. So John is saying, "What kind of exotic love did God bestow on us to make us His sons?" In other words, the love of God that made us sons is alien to the human race, unfamiliar to the human realm, unearthly, and otherworldly. It belongs in another dimension.

Let us illustrate the use of this phrase further. In Matthew 8:23-27 Jesus had a small problem—a storm at sea while He was asleep. When the disciples awoke Him and cried out, "Save us, Lord, we are perishing!" Jesus arose and rebuked the winds and the sea. He stood up and said, "Quiet!" "The men were amazed, and said, 'What kind of a man is this, that even the winds and the sea obey Him?'" (v. 27, emphasis added). Same word. "Where did Jesus come from? What kind of unearthly, otherworldly person is this?" They used it of Jesus, and John used it of God's love.

One further illustration. In 2 Peter 3:10, 11 the apostle said:

> But the day of the Lord will come like a thief, in which the heavens will pass away with a roar and the elements will be destroyed with intense heat, and the earth and its works will be burned up. Since all these things are to be destroyed in this way, what sort of people ought you to be *in holy conduct and godliness*. (emphasis added)

In other words, if you are God's child and you know how it is all going to end, you ought to be an otherworldly, unearthly kind of person. Do you want to attach yourself to something that is going to be burned up? Jesus was an unearthly Person, and we are to be unearthly people.

Now the word translated "love" used throughout 1 John is *agape*. It, too, carries the idea of being unearthly. Human love is object-oriented. In other words, it selects a nice object and loves it. Human love discriminates on the basis of the object. But God's love has nothing to do with the object. God's love is based on God's nature. And that is a foreign, unearthly kind of love, outside our experience. God loves you, not because you attracted His love, but because it was His nature to love. Because you existed, you got loved! Tremendous!

The result of God's wonderful love is that we should be called the "children of God." It is exciting to realize that God is my Father. He is not just my great God somewhere off in the distance; He is near, and He loves me. I can go to Him just as I can to my human father and know that if I ask Him for bread, He is not going to give me a stone, because He loves me. I am His child. In fact, He has even promised that I am a joint heir with Jesus Christ, His Son. Everything He has prepared for Christ, He is going to let me share!

The parable of the prodigal son illustrates this very well. After the son had squandered his inheritance, recognized his sin, and returned home, did his father treat him as a slave? No, but as a son. God made you a son, not a slave. Your relation to Him is that of a child to a loving Father.

John is saying in this text: "This whole confidence, this whole hope I have in the future is based on the love of God—an unearthly love, an otherworldly love, a love beyond what humankind could ever conceive." Then he adds, "For this reason the world does not know us, because it did not know Him." Jesus said that we should not be surprised if the world hates us, because it hated Him (John 15:18-25). Christ was otherworldly. So are we. But how exciting!

Our Hope Is Fulfilled in Christ's Likeness

Imagine that! Someday you are going to be like Christ. "Beloved, now we are children of God" (1 John 3:2). When did you become a child of God? The minute you believed. Are you a child of God now? Absolutely.

Of course, you are not crowned as yet. You still have to struggle with mortal weakness and the devil's crowd. But you are no less a son of God. It is just that God is not finished with you yet. He is a Sculptor who keeps chiseling away as the form He desires emerges. Michelangelo said once, "In every block of stone I see an angel to be liberated." God looks at each of us and says, "There's something in there, and I'm going to get it out."

What is a continuing process now will become an instantaneous accomplishment when Jesus comes. The last part of verse 2 reads, "It has not appeared as yet what we will be. We know that when He appears, we will be like Him, because we will see Him just as He is."

Note the three steps: First, He will appear; then we will see Him as He is; and finally "we will be like Him." That is His plan for us. God is going to make every Christian like Christ. Check out Romans 8:29: "For those whom He foreknew, He also predestined to become conformed to the image of His Son." That is exciting—to know that we will be like Him! John 17:22-24 promises this, as does 1 Corinthians 13:12. But the promise of all promises about seeing Jesus comes to us in Revelation 22:4: "They will see His face, and His name will be on their foreheads." We are going to see Jesus face-to-face for all eternity, and when we see Him, we will be transformed, becoming like Him.

First John 3:2 says we will actually be like Christ. So does Philippians 3:20, 21: "For our citizenship is in heaven, from which also we eagerly wait for a Savior, the Lord Jesus Christ; who will transform the body of our humble state into conformity with the body of His glory, by the exertion of the power that He has even to subject all things to Himself."

The post-Resurrection appearances of our Lord give us suggestions as to what His glorified body is like. It could pass through walls, could appear and reappear as He chose. He could instantly fly to places—to the mountains, right up to heaven. That is the way we will be.

First Corinthians 15 gives us a great deal more information about our future glorified bodies. They will be incorruptible, meaning no decay, no growing old, and no falling apart (v. 42). Our bodies will be glorious, transcending anything we can imagine, and they will be powerful, with all weakness forever behind us. The bodies God will one day give us will be "spiritual"—that is, governed by spirit, not by animal life (v. 44). The kind of body Christ now has, we will one day share.

Our Hope Is Characterized by Purity

"And everyone who has this hope fixed on Him purifies himself, just as He is pure" (1 John 3:3). If you really have this hope and you know you are going to be like Christ, it should change the way you live.

You see, our hope is not just theological—it is moral. It has behavioral consequences. If I really believe in the Second Coming of Christ, if I really believe that He is going to reward His church, if I really believe that He is going to bring me to His judgment seat, then this belief is going to make a big difference in the way I behave.

In the apostle John's day—as in ours—there were people who were saying, "We're Christians! We're Christians!" But a look at their lives disclosed no purity, no righteousness, no love, and no obedience. So John declared, "Write them off. They're wolves in sheep's clothing. They're phonies." The proof of being a Christian is not just having a hope; the proof is having a hope that makes a difference in your life.

The knowledge that you will one day be like Christ should motivate you to become like Him now. We are creatures of motivation, and this is certainly the highest motive to make us live pure lives.

When I used to play football, everyone had to do push-ups at the end of practice sessions. We would—as long as the coach was watching. When he turned his back, however, we would be tempted to lie on the ground. But if he glanced again in our direction—back to action! The very presence of an authority figure changed the way we behaved. That is external motivation.

Jesus is not coming back simply as an authority figure. He is coming back as a loving Savior who desires to reward us and make us like Himself. That should motivate us internally to love and obey Him and to conform ourselves to the purity that is His standard.

There will be times in your Christian experience when you feel like giving up, quitting, climbing out of the arena of life. When that happens, think of that little group of believers—suffering persecution and tribulations—to whom Paul wrote. He reminded them they had been called so that they might "gain the glory of our Lord Jesus Christ" (2 Thessalonians 2:14). He urged them to stand fast on the Word of God.

Then Paul added this benediction, which I echo: "Now may our Lord Jesus Christ Himself and God our Father, who has loved us and given us eternal comfort and good hope by grace, comfort and strengthen your hearts in every good work and word" (vv. 16, 17).

When you're tempted to drop out of the race of faith, hold tight to your hope and think of the poet's encouraging words:

> *Oh, to be like Thee, dear Jesus, my plea,*
> *Just to know Thou art formed fully in me.*
> *On with Thy beauty, Lord, off with my sin,*
> *Fixed on Thy glory Thy likeness to win.*

Oh, to be like Thee, Thine image display,
This is the Spirit's work day after day.
Glory to glory transformed by His grace,
Till in Thy presence I stand face-to-face.

Oh, to be like Thee, Thou lover of men,
Gracious and gentle, compassionate friend.
Merciful Savior, such kindness and care,
Are only mine when Thy likeness I share.

To be like Thee, Jesus!
To be like Thee, Jesus!
For this I live, to this I'll die;
It is my hope, my prayer, my cry.

10

BIBLE STUDY

Unlocking the Library

The Bible is God's final, complete, and authoritative revelation to man. It is our guide for living life, the standard by which we measure our behavior. There may be other things we learn that are helpful, but they don't have the authority that Scripture does. When the Bible speaks, God speaks.

Since that is true, the Bible demands our careful, diligent study. If the Bible is God's Word, if it is our guide in life, we must learn what it says. Not only must we learn what it says, but we must understand what it means by what it says. Knowing what the Bible says will do us little good if we fail to interpret it properly.

WHY STUDY THE BIBLE?

Ours is an entertainment-oriented society. A myriad of different things compete with Bible study for our time. Some Christians spend their time reading all kinds of books besides the Bible. If you go into the average Christian bookstore, you'll find that fiction, personal-experience stories, psychology and self-help manuals, and books about current events far outnumber the commentaries and books on Bible doctrine.

Some of those books may be helpful. Some are written by godly people and are biblically sound. No doubt God often uses them in our lives to promote spiritual growth. But no matter how helpful and biblically sound they might be, they are no substitute for serious Bible study. If we neglect consistent, serious study of God's Word, our spiritual growth will be stunted.

Bible Study Is Necessary for Spiritual Growth

The New Testament repeatedly speaks of Christians as having been born again (John 3:7; 1 Peter 1:3) or as children of God (Romans 8:16; 1 John 3:1). We have been born into the family of God, adopted as His children.

That implies a capacity for spiritual growth. How are we to grow? Peter gives the answer in 1 Peter 2:2: "Like newborn babes, long for the pure milk of the word, so that by it you may grow in respect to salvation." If you don't feed a baby properly, it will not develop and mature. Peter says that in terms of spiritual growth, the same thing is true. Just as a baby grows by taking in milk, so a Christian grows spiritually by taking in the Word.

A graphic illustration of this principle comes from Jeremiah 15:16. "Your words were found and I ate them, and Your words became for me a joy and the delight of my heart." Jeremiah consumed the Word of God, and it brought him great joy.

Paul understood how important it is for believers to feed on the Word of God. He wrote to the Corinthians, "And I, brethren, could not speak to you as to spiritual men, but as to men of flesh, as to babes in Christ. I gave you milk to drink, not solid food; for you were not yet able to receive it. Indeed, even now you are not yet able" (1 Corinthians 3:1, 2). Paul gave the Corinthians milk, not solid food, due to their immaturity. Nevertheless, he did feed them the Word of God.

Paul's metaphorical reference to milk and solid food should not be misunderstood. He's not saying that some parts of Scripture are milk, while others are solid food. Rather, all of the Bible can be either milk or solid food, depending on how deeply you study it. "For God so loved the world, that He gave His only begotten Son, that whoever believes in Him shall not perish, but have eternal life" (John 3:16) might be "milk" for a young Christian. For a mature Christian, with a greater understanding of the love of God, John 3:16 might be "solid food." The Bible contains truths that are so

simple even the youngest Christian can understand them, yet so pro-
found that the most mature believer cannot fully plumb their depths.

Paul exhorted the Colossians, "Therefore as you have received
Christ Jesus the Lord, so walk in Him, having been firmly rooted
and now being built up in Him and established in your faith, just
as you were instructed" (Colossians 2:6, 7). How do Christians
grow? By being built up and established in the faith—the content of
Christianity, biblical doctrine. The more we understand the Bible,
the more established and built up we are.

In his farewell message to the elders of the Ephesian church,
Paul said, "And now I commend you to God and to the word of His
grace, which is able to build you up" (Acts 20:32). It is the Word
that builds us up and causes us to grow spiritually.

Growth is basic to usefulness. Babies are wonderful to have
around, but they're not much help around the house. Unfortunately,
that could also be said of a lot of Christians. Their lack of spiritual
maturity greatly reduces their usefulness to the cause of Christ.

Bible Study Is Necessary for Victory over Sin
Are you experiencing frustration in your battle with sin? Do your
defeats outnumber your victories? Perhaps the problem is that you
are fighting the battle with the wrong weapon. We will never be able
to defeat sin unless we fight it with the Word of God.

All the armor Paul lists in Ephesians 6 is designed for defensive,
protective use—except for one offensive weapon: "the sword of the
Spirit, which is the word of God" (v. 17). What defeats temptation
and sin? Ultimately only the Word of God. The psalmist writes,
"How can a young man keep his way pure? By keeping it according
to Your word. . . . Your word I have treasured in my heart, that
I may not sin against You" (Psalm 119:9, 11). The apostle John
describes spiritual young men as those who overcome the evil one
through the Word of God that abides within them (1 John 2:14).

Knowing the Bible is a wonderful weapon against sin. The more
we affirm biblical truth, the stronger we are against sin. After years
of studying and absorbing the Word of God, I find it has steeled me
against temptation. I can hardly get started in a sin without thinking

of several Bible verses that confront that sin. On the other hand, if you fill your mind with things other than God's Word, the Holy Spirit has nothing of any value to bring to your mind when you're tempted.

Computer people often refer to the acronym GIGO: "Garbage In, Garbage Out." Computers depend entirely on what information is fed into them. Nearly all "computer errors" are actually programming or input errors. Feed bad information or faulty instructions into a computer, and you'll get bad results. The same thing is true in your mind. What you fill your thoughts with will inevitably show up in how you behave. Proverbs 23:7 puts it this way: "For as [a person] thinks within himself, so he is." Filling your mind with the truths of God's Word will result in holiness and godly behavior. Filling your mind with other things will bear corresponding fruit. Jesus expressed the results of a mind not filled with God's truth in Mark 7:21-23: "For from within, out of the heart of men, proceed the evil thoughts, fornications, thefts, murders, adulteries, deeds of coveting and wickedness, as well as deceit, sensuality, envy, slander, pride and foolishness. All these evil things proceed from within and defile the man."

Bible Study Is Necessary for Effective Service

A thorough knowledge of the Bible is absolutely essential for effective spiritual service. The Bible gives us the support and insight we need to handle difficult situations. It also teaches us how to do the Lord's work His way and keeps us from violating His principles for ministry.

In Joshua 1:8, 9 we see how God prepared Joshua for the formidable task that lay before him—the conquest of the Promised Land.

> *"This book of the law shall not depart from your mouth, but you shall meditate on it day and night, so that you may be careful to do according to all that is written in it; for then you will make your way prosperous, and then you will have success. Have I not commanded you? Be strong and courageous! Do not tremble or be dismayed, for the* LORD *your God is with you wherever you go."*

How was Joshua to prepare for his task? Did he need to study management and leadership techniques? Did he need to read a book on how to motivate people? Joshua's first priority was to study and meditate on the Word of God. That, the Lord told him, would bring him success in his ministry.

The apostle Paul, writing to his young protégé Timothy, gave him this wise counsel on how to be a success in the ministry: "In pointing out these things to the brethren, you will be a good servant of Christ Jesus, constantly nourished on the words of the faith and of the sound doctrine which you have been following" (1 Timothy 4:6).

What makes a good minister, or servant, of Christ? It is constant feeding on the Word of God and sound doctrine. When you know the Word of God, you make a good servant of God.

Bible Study Is Necessary for Spiritual Blessing

Most of us would rather be happy than sad. Not many people enjoy being miserable. Life is made up of miserable times and happy times, but I've found that the more I study the Bible, the happier I am, no matter what the circumstances are. The Word of God makes me happy. Psalm 1 describes a happy man as one "who does not walk in the counsel of the wicked, nor stand in the path of sinners, nor sit in the seat of scoffers! But his delight is in the law of the LORD, and in His law he meditates day and night" (vv. 1, 2). A happy person is someone who studies the Bible.

When you come across a sad, miserable Christian, the first thing to check on is the consistency of his Bible study. In my experience as a pastor, I've seen many people who struggled in their Christian walks until they began to regularly study Scripture.

Bible Study Is Necessary to Make Us Effective Counselors

What is the best way to help people who are struggling? By showing them God's solution to their problems. But how can you do that unless you study the Bible? How can you share principles with others that you yourself haven't discovered? A prerequisite for helping others is to know God's Word.

Paul told the Corinthians that God "comforts us in all our

affliction so that we will be able to comfort those who are in any affliction with the comfort with which we ourselves are comforted by God" (2 Corinthians 1:4). Certainly one of the ways God comforted Paul in his trials was through the Scriptures. Paul in turn used what God taught him to minister to others.

Knowledge of Scripture Is Also Essential for Discipling Others

In 2 Timothy 2:2 Paul told Timothy, "The things which you have heard from me in the presence of many witnesses, entrust these to faithful men who will be able to teach others also." Once again we see the truth that we can't pass on to others things we haven't learned ourselves.

If we would be effective in evangelism, we must know the Word. Peter writes, "But sanctify Christ as Lord in your hearts, always being ready to make a defense to everyone who asks you to give an account for the hope that is in you, yet with gentleness and reverence" (1 Peter 3:15). There's nothing more frustrating than not knowing the answers to the questions people ask us or to know the answer but not remember a verse that supports that answer. Knowing Scripture is crucial to effective evangelism.

HOW TO STUDY THE BIBLE

Before we can study the Bible, there is a necessary first step of preparation. That is found in 1 Peter 2. Verse 2, as we have seen, speaks of the Christian's taking in the Word of God. Verse 1 tells us what we must do first: "Therefore, putting aside all malice and all deceit and hypocrisy and envy and all slander . . ." James agrees that sin must be put away if the Word is to benefit us: "Therefore, putting aside all filthiness and all that remains of wickedness, in humility receive the word implanted, which is able to save your souls" (James 1:21).

What does that tell us? Before we can study the Bible with any profit, we must deal with sin. An excellent way to begin our Bible study is with a time of confession of sin and prayer for God's guidance. Then what?

Read the Bible

Become familiar with what it says. This is the necessary first step in Bible study, and it brings blessing from God. Some people avoid the book of Revelation, thinking it is too difficult to understand. Yet God promises that those who read and obey Revelation will be happy: "Blessed [happy] is he who reads and those who hear the words of the prophecy, and heed the things which are written in it" (Revelation 1:3).

I used to struggle with retaining what I read in the Bible. I'd read a passage, and by the next day I'd forget what I'd read. I'd read through a book and not know much about it when I finished. I was wasting a lot of time and effort and not really accomplishing very much.

I decided that the best way for me to learn the Bible was to read it repetitiously. Isaiah said we learn "line on line, line on line, a little here, a little there" (28:13). It's like studying for a test in school. You don't just read the material once; you go over it repeatedly.

I recommend beginning with a fairly short New Testament book (in chapter 1 I described how I began using this method with 1 John). Read it straight through at one sitting. Read it in the Bible you use all the time. (If you're not sure what Bible translation to use, I recommend the *New American Standard Bible*, the *New King James Version*, or the *New International Version*.) Do that every day for thirty days, and at the end of that time you will know what's in that book. In fact, you will even be able to visualize where passages are on their respective pages (which is why you should do your reading in the same Bible each day). Writing down the theme of each chapter on a three-by-five card will also help you to master the contents of the book. You may find (as I did) that thirty days isn't enough. You may find yourself so excited at what you are learning that you want to extend your reading to sixty or even ninety days.

What happens when you come to a longer New Testament book, such as one of the Gospels? You divide it into shorter sections and read each of them in turn for thirty days. For example, if you choose to read the Gospel of John, you would read chapters

1 through 7 for thirty days, then chapters 8 through 14 for the next thirty days, and finally chapters 15 through 21 for the last thirty days. In ninety days you will have read John's Gospel thirty times.

I suggest you continue that pattern of alternately reading short and long books. In a couple of years you can read the entire New Testament through thirty times. Since you're going to read the Bible for the rest of your life, you should read it in a way that will help you retain what you read.

That probably isn't the best approach to use in studying the Old Testament. Since the Old Testament is largely narrative history and poetry, each book doesn't need to be read repetitiously. Instead, just read through the Old Testament consecutively, from beginning to end. Once you have read it, go back and start again at the beginning. That should be a lifetime practice. There are several Bible-reading plans available that guide you through the entire Old Testament in one year.

As you systematically read through the Bible, you will become increasingly familiar with its contents. You will be able to cross-reference passages on your own, without being so dependent on a concordance. Often a topic or theme in one passage will remind you of a similar theme in another passage. You will gradually develop a good understanding of what the Bible teaches on various topics.

Study the Bible

Reading the Bible is a crucial first step, and we will learn much from doing it. We must not stop there, however. We need to dig beneath the surface of Scripture by doing serious Bible study. There are various methods of Bible study.

You might, for example, study a Bible topic. Or you could study all the prayers of the Bible. You could begin in Genesis and find every passage where someone prays. Then you could note who was praying, what his or her request was, and how it was answered. Or you could study just the prayers of Paul or any other biblical character. You could study forgiveness, judgment, or any topic you can think of. A topical index, such as *Nave's*

Topical Bible or my *MacArthur Topical Bible,* is very helpful in doing topical studies. An exhaustive concordance is also useful, containing far more entries than the concordance in the back of your Bible. The three best ones based on the *King James Version* text are *Strong's Exhaustive Concordance of the Bible, Young's Analytical Concordance to the Holy Bible,* and *Cruden's Complete Concordance of the Old and New Testaments.* If you use the *New American Standard Bible,* you'll want to get the *New American Standard Exhaustive Concordance of the Bible,* or if you use the *New International Version,* the *NIV Exhaustive Concordance.*

Another way to study the Bible is to study Bible biographies. You could study one of the great men of the Old Testament such as Elijah, David, or Joseph, or a New Testament figure such as Peter or Paul. You could even study someone not as well-known, such as Andrew. We can learn much of value from seeing how those men lived their lives and how God dealt with them. Bible encyclopedias such as the *Zondervan Pictorial Encyclopedia of the Bible,* the *Baker Encyclopedia of the Bible,* or the *International Standard Bible Encyclopedia* contain helpful articles on Bible characters.

Perhaps the most important method of Bible study is to study a passage. After you've read through a book thirty times, you'll have a good grasp of its contents. Outline the book and study each section of the outline. That is essentially what I do in my preparation for preaching.

All serious study, of course, begins with reading. Saturate your mind with the contents of the passage. Read it in several different English translations, since each version will bring out different shades of the meaning of the original text.

As you read a passage, look for the key concepts—the main truths it is teaching. Those will become clearer the more you read the passage. When you discover them, write them down, along with any questions or problems that you come across. Try to learn as much as you can from the passage itself before you turn to outside sources. Finally, put together a preliminary outline of the passage.

The next step is to study the passage verse by verse, using commentaries, word studies, Bible dictionaries or encyclopedias, and any other reference tool that might be helpful. Reading what godly scholars have said about a passage will help keep us from misinterpreting it. Be sure to take notes as you read.

The last step is to prepare a final outline, taking into account all the material you've gathered during your study. If you are going to teach the passage, you will want to find ways to illustrate and apply the truths you have found. I try to use biblical illustrations whenever possible, since Scripture is best explained by other Scripture. A helpful tool in finding other passages with similar themes is *The Treasury of Scripture Knowledge*. This book contains cross-references for nearly every verse in the Bible. It is similar to the marginal references found in many Bibles, but far more extensive.

Teach the Bible

Don't keep what you've learned to yourself. Find someone else and teach what you've learned. If you are married, share with your spouse. If you have children, teach them. Find someone you can disciple. Even if you're a new Christian, find someone who knows less than you, and teach that person what you've learned. Being responsible to teach others is a strong motivation for our own study. Undoubtedly the greatest practical incentive I have for studying the Bible is my responsibility for preaching on Sundays.

Be Accountable

Find someone who will hold you accountable to study the Bible, especially if you don't teach the Bible on a regular basis. Find someone who models biblical truths in his or her life, and pattern your life after that person's.

Hear the Word Taught

Attend a church where the Word is honored and taught. Listen to tapes of gifted Bible expositors. Read the sermons of great preachers of the past. That cannot substitute for your own personal study, but it is a necessary supplement to it. Too many Christians are caught up in Christian entertainment. They go from one event to another, watching Christian films, attending Christian concerts, or pursuing some Christian "celebrity." Somehow they never seem to submit themselves to systematic teaching of the Word of God. Don't let pursuit of entertainment keep you from receiving the biblical instruction that is essential for spiritual growth.

The Bible is central to the Christian life. It is God's infallible, inerrant, complete, authoritative, and sufficient Word to us. It is our source of truth, happiness, victory, growth, power, and guidance. It is an absolutely essential key to spiritual growth.

11

FELLOWSHIP

Unlocking the Family Room

The Bible uses several metaphors for the church. It pictures the church as a flock, with Christ as its Shepherd (John 10:14). It views us as branches of Christ, the Vine (John 15:5), subjects of Christ's kingdom (John 18:36, 37), and children of God's family (John 1:12). While all those metaphors are also used in the Old Testament to describe God's relationship with Israel, there is one that is unique to the church. That is the concept of the church as a body, with Christ as its head (Colossians 1:18).

All believers become part of the body of Christ at the moment of salvation, through the baptism of the Holy Spirit. The baptism of the Holy Spirit is not a post-salvation, "second blessing" experience, but rather, the only means of entrance into the body. Paul states that clearly in 1 Corinthians 12:13: "For by one Spirit we were all baptized into one body, whether Jews or Greeks, whether slaves or free, and we were all made to drink of one Spirit." When you were saved, the Holy Spirit placed you into the body of Christ. You became a member of the church.

SALVATION: ENTRANCE TO THE BODY

It's very important that we understand what takes place at salvation. Perhaps we can best understand the riches of our salvation by looking at several key terms.

Reconciliation. Reconciliation is "the bringing together of two parties that are in dispute; particularly, Christ's bringing God and man together, the result of which is salvation."[1] Man and God are separated by sin: "Your iniquities have made a separation between you and your God" (Isaiah 59:2). Christ's death on the cross has reconciled us to God.

Ephesians 2:11-16 is a good illustration of this truth. Verses 11, 12 describe our condition before salvation: "Therefore remember that formerly you, the Gentiles in the flesh . . . were at that time separate from Christ, excluded from the commonwealth of Israel, and strangers to the covenants of promise, having no hope and without God in the world." An unbeliever is cut off from God's Son, God's people, God's covenants, and God's presence. He is truly without hope.

Mercifully, God did not leave us in that hopeless condition. Verses 13-16 go on to describe our condition after salvation:

> But now in Christ Jesus you who formerly were far off have been brought near by the blood of Christ. For He Himself is our peace, who made both groups into one and broke down the barrier of the dividing wall, by abolishing in His flesh the enmity, which is the Law of commandments contained in ordinances, so that in Himself He might make the two into one new man, thus establishing peace, and might reconcile them both in one body to God through the cross, by it having put to death the enmity.

Christ's atoning death on the cross accomplished our reconciliation. When we put our faith in Christ, the barrier between us and God, which was caused by sin, is removed. All genuine believers, regardless of their denomination, are one with each other through their union with the Lord Jesus Christ (1 Corinthians 6:17).

Jesus Christ came into the world to bring peace between God and man, who were enemies because of man's sin. Christ accomplished that through His sacrificial death on the cross. Truly "He Himself is our peace" (Ephesians 2:14).

Justification. Justification is "the act of God in bringing sinners into a new covenant relationship with himself through the forgiveness of sins. . . . It is a declarative act of God by which he establishes persons as righteous."[2] In justification, guilty sinners are declared righteous by God. God is able to be "just and the justifier of the one who has faith in Jesus" (Romans 3:26) because the death of Jesus paid the price for our sin (Romans 5:9). The ground of our justification is not our good works. Justification is a gift of God (Romans 3:24) and comes through faith alone (Romans 3:28).

Justification must not be severed from sanctification. Justification will inevitably manifest itself in the changed life of an individual. Paul tells us in 2 Corinthians 5:17, "If anyone is in Christ, he is a new creature; the old things passed away; behold, new things have come." As a result of our salvation, we are to "walk in newness of life" (Romans 6:4).

Regeneration. Regeneration may be defined as "that act of God by which the principle of the new life is implanted in man, and the governing disposition of the soul is made holy."[3] Another name for regeneration is the new birth. The Bible refers to it in such passages as John 1:12, 13; 3:3, 6; and 1 Peter 1:3, 23.

A good illustration of regeneration is found in Ephesians 2. Verse 1 says that before you were saved, "you were dead in your trespasses and sins." Before your salvation, you were spiritually dead. You were unable to respond to spiritual stimuli, just as a physically dead person cannot respond to physical stimuli.

That reality was graphically illustrated to me through a tragic incident that took place many years ago. I was sitting in my office one day when someone began pounding frantically on the door. I opened it to find a little boy who lived in a house just down the street from the church. He pleaded with me through his tears, "Please come and help us. My baby sister just died." I hurried after him as he ran down the street to his house. When I arrived, his distraught mother pointed to a bedroom and said, "My baby is dead." I entered the bedroom, and there on the bed was a baby, about three or four months old. I asked the woman if she had tried to revive the baby, and she said she had. Sobbing uncontrollably, she picked up the limp, lifeless little form and kissed and stroked it. Soon the paramedics arrived, but they too were unable to revive the baby.

Although the love of a mother for her child is perhaps the most powerful of all human emotions, even that was unable to elicit a response from the baby. To be physically dead renders one incapable of responding, no matter what the stimuli.

Spiritual death has a similar effect. To be spiritually dead is to be unable to respond to God. That's why Paul says that before our salvation, we "lived in the lusts of our flesh, indulging the desires of the flesh and of the mind, and were by nature children of wrath, even as the rest" (Ephesians 2:3). God's love drew no response from us.

That all changed after our salvation: "But God, being rich in mercy, because of His great love with which He loved us, even when we were dead in our transgressions, made us alive together with Christ" (vv. 4, 5). Being spiritually dead, we were helpless (Romans 5:6), unable to change our condition. Because of God's great love and mercy, He took the initiative and granted us new life in Christ. As a result, we are now spiritually alive. We have an awareness of God's presence, and we commune with Him in prayer. We hear Him speak to our hearts through His Word.

Among the many blessings of salvation, then, are reconciliation, justification, and regeneration. Those truly are blessings, "far more abundantly beyond all that we ask or think" (Ephesians 3:20). Yet, to all that God adds one more blessing. He places those reconciled, justified, and regenerate individuals into the church, the body of Christ. In Paul's words, we are "in Christ" (Romans 8:1; 1 Corinthians 1:30). And that grants to us a whole new set of privileges.

THE PRIVILEGES OF THE BODY

To be "in Christ" means you are so identified with Him that God always views you in connection with Christ. You don't have a spiritual identity apart from Christ. That's why God can impute righteousness to you and forgive your sins, because He sees you in Christ. That's why Paul can say that we are "fellow heirs with Christ" (Romans 8:17). All our spiritual blessings come to us through our union with Christ: "Blessed be the God and Father of our Lord Jesus Christ, who has blessed us with every spiritual blessing in the heavenly places in Christ" (Ephesians 1:3).

Through our union with Christ, we are adopted by God. Ephesians 1:5 says, "He predestined us to adoption as sons through Jesus Christ to Himself." As a result, we have an intimate relationship with Him. Paul says in Romans 8:15 that we refer to God as "Abba"—the Aramaic equivalent of our term *Daddy*.

Our identification with Christ is also one guarantee that we can never lose our salvation. Because we are in Christ, we have "become the righteousness of God in Him" (2 Corinthians 5:21). God has imparted Christ's righteousness to us, and as a result we are completely forgiven. God has predestined those who are in Christ "to become conformed to the image of His Son" (Romans 8:29). Verse 30 shows us the unbreakable link between predestination and glorification: All who are predestined are eventually glorified; none are lost along the way (see also John 6:39). That marvelous truth caused Paul to cry out triumphantly, "Who will bring a charge against God's elect? God is the one who justifies; who is the one who condemns? Christ Jesus is He who died, yes, rather who was raised, who is at the right hand of God, who also intercedes for us" (Romans 8:33, 34). The Father will never condemn us, and neither will Christ. Our salvation is secure.

Not only is our salvation secure, it is also complete. Colossians 2:10 tells us that "in Him [Christ] you have been made complete," while 2 Peter 1:3 informs us that "His divine power has granted to us everything pertaining to life and godliness." We lack nothing.

New believers aren't spiritual pollywogs. They don't add new parts as they grow and mature. Just as a newborn baby is fully formed but needs to grow, so also does a newborn Christian need to "grow in the grace and knowledge of our Lord and Savior Jesus Christ" (2 Peter 3:18). But all the parts are there from the beginning. We are complete in Christ.

What should be our response to all the blessings that are ours in Christ? We must live lives consistent with the reality of who we are in Christ.

I have a friend who played football for the Green Bay Packers during their glory years under Vince Lombardi. He told me there was something about putting on a Packer uniform that motivated players to play above their normal level. They wanted to uphold the tradition of that team. That's how it should be for Christians. Our Father is the sovereign ruler of the universe, and we must live lives that reflect favorably on Him. That's why Paul exhorted the Ephesians to "walk in a manner worthy of the calling with which you have been called" (Ephesians 4:1).

God sees us as perfect and complete in Christ. Spiritual growth does not affect that. Spiritual growth takes place as we live more consistently with who we are in Christ. The Christian life is the process of becoming what we are.

THE GIFTS OF THE BODY

There is a real unity in the body of Christ. Although the true church is made up of a diverse group of people, we are one body. In the body of Christ, Paul told the Galatians, "There is neither Jew nor Greek, there is neither slave nor free man, there is neither male nor female; for you are all one in Christ Jesus" (Galatians 3:28). But along with that unity comes a diversity of spiritual gifts. Each member of the body is uniquely gifted by God, and if one member doesn't use his gift, the body suffers.

There are many gifts listed in Scripture, including prophecy, teaching, faith, wisdom, knowledge, discernment of spirits, mercy, exhortation, giving, administration, miracles, healings, tongues, and interpretation of tongues. (The last four were temporary sign gifts given to the early church and are not operative today.)[4] Every Christian has certain gifts, as 1 Corinthians 12:7-11 makes clear. Each believer is responsible to use those gifts in service so that the other members of the body can benefit (v. 7). I mentioned in an earlier chapter that it would be silly for someone with the gift of teaching to stand in front of a mirror and teach himself. It would be equally silly to imagine someone with the gift of mercy or giving who uses his gift only on himself. Contrary to much popular teaching today, no spiritual gift was ever intended for private edification.

What is a spiritual gift? It is not a human ability or talent. You may be a natural athlete, musician, artist, or writer, but those are not spiritual gifts. Although you may express your spiritual gifts through those abilities, the two are not the same. In contrast to a natural talent, a spiritual gift is a God-given channel through which the Holy Spirit ministers.

Spiritual gifts are not obtained by seeking or "tarrying." We cannot use gimmicks or techniques to get the ones we want. Nor is there any one gift that all Christians can have (see 1 Corinthians 12:29, 30). Spiritual gifts are distributed in the body of the Holy Spirit according to His sovereign will (1 Corinthians 12:11). And as the analogy of the human body for the church makes clear, all the gifts are important (1 Corinthians 12:20-25). Possession of a certain spiritual gift does not mean someone is on a higher level of spirituality.

How do you discover your spiritual gift? Simply live a Spirit-filled life and see how God uses you.

THE FELLOWSHIP OF THE BODY

Closely related to the topic of spiritual gifts is fellowship. In fact, there can be no biblical fellowship apart from the ministry of spiritual gifts. The fellowship of the body is the mutual care and concern its members have for each other. That care and concern is expressed in the "one another" passages of the New Testament. We are to confess our sins one to another (James 5:16), build up one another (1 Thessalonians 5:11), bear one another's burdens (Galatians 6:2), pray for one another (James 5:16), be kind to one another (Ephesians 4:32), submit to one another (Ephesians 5:21), show hospitality to one another (1 Peter 4:9), serve one another (Galatians 5:13), comfort one another (1 Thessalonians 4:18), restore one another (Galatians 6:1), forgive one another (Colossians 3:13), admonish one another (Romans 15:14), teach one another (Colossians 3:16), encourage one another (Hebrews 3:13), and above all, love one another (1 Peter 1:22; 1 John 4:7, 11). Obviously, there's a lot more to biblical fellowship than red punch and stale cookies in the basement of the church fellowship hall! True fellowship takes place when Christians come together to minister to one another in the power of the Holy Spirit.

In a normal, healthy human body, all the parts work together. If they don't, that body is disabled, unable to function normally. No single part functions independently of the rest. So it is also in the body of Christ. All the members must work together if the body is to function normally. And no member was meant to function in isolation from the rest of the body; the New Testament knew nothing of Christians who weren't part of a local assembly. God never intended the church to be a place where lonely people come on Sunday, sit alone among the crowd, and leave, still lonely and hurting. Rather, in the church warm, intimate fellowship takes place. Fellowship is essential both for the church as a whole and for each individual member.

When each member functions properly, the body of Christ is strong and healthy. And that will be a powerful witness that the world can't help noticing.

WITNESSING

Unlocking the Nursery

Quite a few years ago I saw an attempted murder. Two men severely beat a third man, and I intervened and tried to stop them. When the police arrived, they asked if I would testify against the two men. I agreed to do so and eventually was called as a witness for the prosecution at their trial. After being sworn in, the prosecuting attorney asked me to tell the court three things: what I saw, what I heard, and what I felt.

That's a good definition of a witness. A witness tells what he sees, hears, and feels. Such was the testimony the apostle John bore of Jesus in 1 John 1:1, 3: "What was from the beginning, what we have heard, what we have seen with our eyes, what we have looked at and touched with our hands, concerning the Word of Life . . . what we have seen and heard we proclaim to you also." That's what a Christian witness is—someone who tells others of his or her experience with Christ.

The Bible doesn't view witnessing as optional in the Christian life. Such passages as Matthew 28:19, 20 and Acts 1:8 make it clear that all believers are responsible to be witnesses for Christ. You don't have to be well-versed in all the intricacies of theology to be an effective witness. The blind man healed by Jesus in John 9 didn't know how to answer all the theological questions posed to him by the Pharisees, but he could say, "One thing I do know, that though I was blind, now I see" (v. 25). He was able to tell what Jesus had done for him. That's something all Christians, regardless of how much theology and apologetics they know, can do. We can all share what Christ has done in our lives.

Witnesses in a courtroom don't always present their testimony in an orderly manner. They often share things that are irrelevant. But a good attorney will take that testimony and apply it to the case being tried. The Holy Spirit will do the same thing with our testimony. Some of what we say may be right on target; some may not. We have the confidence, however, that the Holy Spirit will take our witness and use it to accomplish His purposes. The Holy Spirit uses our testimonies to build His case for Christ.

All Christians are witnesses. You can't say, "I hope someday to study theology and apologetics so I can witness for Christ." If you are a Christian, you have witnessed what Christ has done in your life. The only question is whether you're willing to give your testimony. The victim in the attempted murder I witnessed was too frightened to testify. He certainly was a witness; he knew perfectly well what had happened to him. But his refusal to testify meant that his testimony was useless in bringing those criminals to justice. Similarly, our testimony of what Christ has done for us is useless if we don't share it. Being a witness is not always easy. Witnesses sometimes face the threat of retaliation from those they testify against. As Christians, we face the possibility that we may be ridiculed or ostracized by those with whom we share Christ. Most of us care more about protecting ourselves than proclaiming Him. But if we are to be effective witnesses for Jesus Christ, we must care more about what the world thinks of Jesus than what it thinks of us.

THE CORPORATE TESTIMONY OF THE CHURCH

Commenting on the importance of the corporate testimony of the church, Gene Getz has written:

> Corporate evangelism is basic to personal evangelism. In the New Testament the functioning body of Christ set the stage for individual witness. This is why Jesus said, "Love one another,

so that all men will know that you are My disciples." This is why Paul said, "Love your neighbor as yourself" (Ro 13:9), and why Peter exhorted believers to keep their "behavior excellent among the Gentiles" (1 Pet 2:12). Personal evangelism takes on unusual significance against the backdrop of a mature body of local believers—Christians who are making an impact on their communities, because of their integrity (1 Th 4:11-12); their unselfish behavior (Ro 13:7); their orderly conduct (1 Co 10:31-33); their wisdom (Col 4:6); their diligence [Galatians 6:9]; their humility (1 Pet 2:18); and yet, their forthright testimony for Jesus Christ (1 Pet 3:15).

It is difficult to witness in isolation. It is often necessary, but God's general plan is that community evangelism be carried out in the context of dynamic Christianity, and vigorous body life.

United in functioning in all of its parts, the local church can make a powerful impact upon a pagan community. Then it is not so much the extrovertish individuals who are often glamorized as the "most spiritual" because they witness, but it becomes a ministry of the total body of Christ, in which all share the joy and reward of those who have the privilege of "drawing the net" for Christ.[1]

The witness of a church to its community both reflects and affects the testimonies of its individual members.

Sometimes the testimony of a church affects the testimony of its members. Once a church in our area held a dance. Someone spiked the punch, and the church leaders got drunk. One woman even did a striptease. Needless to say, the negative publicity surrounding that incident destroyed that church's reputation. You can imagine the difficulty those church members had in sharing the Gospel after that incident. Once the person they were witnessing to learned what church they attended, the conversation ended. The credibility of the organization to which you belong is very important to your personal testimony.

The actions of an individual, on the other hand, can adversely affect the testimony of an entire congregation. I was appalled by an incident that took place in our church some years ago. A man who attended Grace Community invited an attorney friend to attend one of our Sunday services. "I'd never attend that church," the attorney replied. "The most crooked lawyer I know goes to your church." Here was a case where one man's sinful lifestyle affected the testimony of an entire church. That incident disturbed me so much that the following Sunday I related the incident to our congregation and asked that lawyer, whoever he was, to either get his life together or leave our church.

THE TESTIMONY OF INDIVIDUAL BELIEVERS

Your effectiveness as a witness for Jesus Christ is affected not only by the corporate testimony of your church, but also by the credibility of your own life. If your behavior doesn't back up what you say, people will notice, and your testimony will not be believable.

Jesus said in Matthew 23:2, 3, "The scribes and the Pharisees have seated themselves in the chair of Moses; therefore all that they tell you, do and observe, but do not do according to their deeds; for they say things and do not do them." They were hypocrites. They said one thing and did another. We must not be like that. People need to see in our lives the reality of what we profess.

I once preached a message at a local prison. Afterwards, one of the inmates came up to me and said, "That was really great. I'm glad to see a brother in Christ. You know, I'm in the Lord's work too." He told me the name of the Christian organization he worked for. Somewhat puzzled, I asked him what he was doing in jail. "Oh," he replied, "I got several traffic tickets, and I never paid any of them, so I was sentenced to ninety days in jail."

I reminded him of Peter's words in 1 Peter 2:13-15: "Submit yourselves for the Lord's sake to every human institution, whether to a king as the one in authority, or to governors as sent by him for the punishment of evildoers and the praise of those who do right. For such is the will of God that by doing right you may silence the ignorance of foolish men." Then I said to him, "Do the rest of us a favor, and don't tell anybody you're a Christian. We don't need that kind of publicity." That really shook him up, but then I had an opportunity to talk to him about the importance of credibility.

You may not be in prison, but there are other less obvious ways that your lifestyle can undermine your testimony. Perhaps you aren't diligent in giving your employer a good day's work. Maybe you talk to others about Christ when you should be working. If your employer and the other employees at your job know that, your testimony will be discredited. Or if you're a student and get caught cheating on an exam, who will listen when you share Christ? Better to fail the exam than to bring reproach on the cause of Christ!

Don't allow your lifestyle to undermine your testimony and the testimony of other Christians. The apostle Peter gives us some wise counsel in his first epistle: "Such is the will of God that by doing right you may silence the ignorance of foolish men" (2:15); "keep a good conscience so that in the thing in which you are slandered, those who revile your good behavior in Christ will be put to shame" (3:16). Don't let anyone be turned off to the Gospel by your lifestyle.

OUR WITNESS IS DEPENDENT ON THE HOLY SPIRIT

People are not saved because of your testimony. They're not saved because you argue them into silence or because you use a clever "sales pitch" to present the Gospel. No one has ever been saved, or ever will be, apart from the working of the Holy Spirit. Although the apostle Paul shared the Gospel with Lydia, she was not saved until "the Lord opened her heart to respond to the things spoken by Paul" (Acts 16:14). It is the Holy Spirit who will "convict the world concerning sin and righteousness and judgment" (John 16:8). Even knowledge of biblical truths will not save anyone, apart from the work of the Holy Spirit (1 Corinthians 2:14).

That's a liberating truth. Sharing the Gospel would be a terrible burden if people's salvation depended on our persuasiveness. How comforting to know that we are responsible only to be diligent and faithful and to allow the Holy Spirit to use us. People sometimes ask me if I'm disappointed whenever people don't get saved in response to my preaching. I am disappointed for their sake; yet I know that I have been called to preach the Gospel, not to save people. That's the work of the Holy Spirit. All you and I can do is be faithful witnesses for Jesus Christ and allow the sovereign Holy Spirit to do His work.

SOME PRACTICAL TIPS FOR WITNESSING[2]

Witnessing to others about Christ can nevertheless be an intimidating task. Here are some practical steps to help you get started.

Begin by Preparing Your Testimony

I recommend that you write out your testimony. That will enable you to structure it in a clear, orderly manner. Review it often to keep it fresh in your mind.

What kind of structure should a coherent testimony have? Begin by relating your dissatisfaction with life before your salvation. That's something most unbelievers can relate to because they're unhappy too. Look for an opening in conversations when people express dissatisfaction with their life. Mention that you used to feel that way too, and then share your testimony.

The next step is to explain your conversion. Tell how Christ replaced your dissatisfaction with His peace and contentment. Be sure to use Scripture to lay a biblical foundation for your experience.

Then explain what happened after you were converted. Tell how your desires, goals, and priorities changed. Let them know that you now have a whole different perspective on life.

Make sure that you clearly explain the Gospel, from the Bible. Express clearly the biblical truths that all people are sinners, justly condemned by a righteous God, and that salvation comes only through faith in Christ, not by doing good works. Make clear that true repentance means being willing to forsake a sinful lifestyle and live in obedience to Christ.

Then look for opportunities to share your testimony. Peter said, "Sanctify Christ as Lord in your hearts, always being ready to make a defense to everyone who asks you to give an account for the hope that is in you, yet with gentleness and reverence" (1 Peter 3:15).

When you share your testimony, it is important to give the one you're talking to an opportunity to respond. You might ask, "Can you think of any reason why you wouldn't want to receive Christ right now?" The answer you get will demonstrate whether the person is ready to receive Christ or is in need of further teaching and exhortation.

Be Familiar with the Available Resources

A printed tract can be a useful tool in personal evangelism. There are many available, including:

Who Do You Think I Am? (Panorama City, Calif.: Grace to You, 1991).

The Real Purpose of Life (Oklahoma City: Max D. Barnett, 1967).

Life's Most Important Question (Winona Lake, Ind.: BMH, 1975).

There are many others as well. Make sure you choose one that clearly and accurately presents the Gospel. Become familiar with it yourself before you use it in a witnessing situation.

If you have the opportunity, take a class in personal evangelism, such as Evangelism Explosion. There are some excellent manuals on how to witness. One of the best is *Tell the Truth* by Will Metzger (Downers Grove, Ill.: InterVarsity Press, 1981). Learning effective principles of personal evangelism can be very helpful. Make sure the training you receive or the books you read teach you a biblically sound method of evangelism. Far too much evangelism today is man-centered, not God-centered.

Be familiar, too, with books that give evidences for the truth of Christianity and answer objections that nonbelievers often raise. Two helpful works, among many others, are Josh McDowell, *Evidence That Demands a Verdict*, Vol. 1 (San Bernardino, Calif.: Here's Life Publishers, 1986) and R. C. Sproul, *Reason to Believe* (Grand Rapids, Mich.: Zondervan Publishing House, 1982).

Formulate some questions to use in turning a conversation to spiritual matters. Be sensitive and tactful in how you introduce the Gospel into a conversation. Having some questions in mind that you can use when the opportunity arises is helpful. For example, you might ask someone, "Who do you think Jesus Christ is?" Or, "Do you believe it is possible to be absolutely sure of going to heaven? How do you think a person can have that kind of certainty?" Questions like those can be helpful in turning the conversation toward the Gospel. They can also provide you with good insight into a person's spiritual condition.

Finally, be alert for opportunities. A man I know once asked an airline flight attendant what she would do if the plane they were on lost power and crashed into a mountain. Startled, she replied, "Sir, why would you ask a question like that?" He answered, "I just wondered what you would do if you suddenly stood face-to-face with God and He asked you, 'What right do you have to enter heaven?'" She thought about that for a while and finally admitted, "I don't know." With that as an opening, he proceeded to lead her to Christ.

THE IMPORTANCE OF FOLLOW-UP

Our responsibility to those we lead to Christ doesn't end with their conversion. Rather, our goal is to disciple them and bring them to the level of maturity that will allow them to make disciples of their own (2 Timothy 2:2). Jesus charged us to make disciples of those we evangelize (Matthew 28:19, 20). If at all possible, you should establish a discipling relationship with those you lead to Christ. If you can't, try to refer them to someone who can. At the very least, point them to good books and tapes that will help them grow in Christ.

How do you disciple someone? You meet with him regularly and teach him both doctrinal and practical truths from the Bible. Be concerned about his life, and warn him of the consequences if he continues in sin. If the person you are discipling has problems handling money, teach him biblical principles relating to finances. If he struggles with lust, teach him biblical principles for handling temptation. Whatever areas of his life need work, share with him biblical truths that apply. Admonish him if he persists in those sins. Be sure to set an example of godly living in your own life that he can follow. Otherwise your lifestyle will undermine the truth you are teaching him. Above all, love him. Serve him with a sense of humility. Make yourself available to him. Be his friend.

THE URGENCY OF WITNESSING

Some Christians are afraid to confront unbelievers with the Gospel because they are afraid to shake them up. But how much more shaken are they going to be when they realize too late that they don't know the truth? They *need* to be shaken up. Speaking of the urgency of reaching the lost, Jesus said in Matthew 9:37, 38, "The harvest is plentiful, but the workers are few. Therefore beseech the Lord of the harvest to send out workers into His harvest."

Are you one of the Lord's harvesters?

DISCERNMENT

Locking the Security Gate

About ten years ago I drove across the southern states, ministering in some remote areas. One afternoon as I was driving with a fellow pastor through Arkansas, I saw a crudely painted sign advertising handmade quilts. I was interested in purchasing a quilt for my wife, so we stopped to see what might be available. The house was very old and rustic. A woman answered the door and, on learning I was interested in her quilts, enthusiastically invited us in.

Her husband was seated in front of a television, watching a religious program. Stacked around the living room were books, videotapes, and piles of literature. The woman showed me several quilts, then went into another room to get her favorite quilt, leaving me and my friend with her husband.

"Are you believers?" I asked.

"Believers in what?" he replied.

"Believers in Christ," I answered.

"Oh, sure," he told me. Then he showed us his collection of materials. Much of it was solid biblical material, but he also had quite a lot of literature from Jehovah's Witnesses, Mormonism, Scientology, the Unitarian Fellowship, and the Baha'i faith. He was evidently on the mailing list of every major television preacher as well. "We find some good in all of it," he told us.

By then the woman had returned with her favorite quilt. It was, frankly, somewhat unbecoming, made of oddly shaped pieces of diverse fabrics stitched together in no particular pattern. The other quilts she had showed me were far more attractive, and I purchased one of them I especially liked.

After we left, it occurred to me that the woman's prize quilt was a perfect metaphor for the couple's theological outlook. Utterly undiscerning, they were stitching together a unique religion out of scraps cut from every source they could find.

Sadly, those people are not terribly different from the average religious person in our culture—reading, listening to tapes, watching television with little or no discernment, just patching together some amorphous kind of belief system that has little rhyme or reason.

In 1 Thessalonians 5:21, 22 the apostle Paul confronts that mentality: "Examine everything carefully; hold fast to that which is good; abstain from every form of evil." That's one of the basic truths of godly living and a vital key to any level of spiritual maturity.

Unfortunately, in recent years the church has been plagued by an almost inexhaustible gullibility. Preposterous varieties of aberrant teaching wreak havoc among those who call themselves Christians. Confusion and error run rampant. Very few believers seem to have the discernment to differentiate between truth and heresy. Chaos threatens to overwhelm the church. As a result, biblical Christianity is fighting for its very life.

Bad decisions, faulty reasoning, superficial understanding, widespread ignorance, shallow commitment, and poor knowledge of the Scriptures have always troubled the church. In fact, over the ages these internal problems have contributed more to the church's woes than all the external attacks combined. Persecutions have taken their toll, but internal chaos and division over doctrine have left the most scars.

Satan, disguised as an angel of light, wants to confuse the people of God (2 Corinthians 11:13-15). Scripture warns repeatedly of "deceitful spirits and doctrines of demons" (1 Timothy 4:1), "destructive heresies" (2 Peter 2:1), "myths" (1 Timothy 1:4; 2 Timothy 4:4; Titus 1:14), "perverse things" (Acts 20:30), "commandments and teachings of men" (Colossians 2:22; see also Titus 1:14), "foolish and ignorant speculations" (2 Timothy 2:23), "worldly fables" (1 Timothy 4:7), false knowledge and "empty chatter" (1 Timothy

6:20), "philosophy and empty deception" and "the tradition of men" (Colossians 2:8). All of these are pitfalls for Christians.

Jesus warned of "wolves . . . in sheep's clothing" (Matthew 7:15). Paul told the Ephesian elders, "After my departure savage wolves will come in among you, not sparing the flock" (Acts 20:29). And he wrote to warn Timothy, "Evil men and impostors will proceed from bad to worse, deceiving and being deceived" (2 Timothy 3:13).

No one who understands Scripture and is aware of all those warnings about error should ever be so credulous as to look at the various teachings floating around and say, "There's good in all of them." We cannot for a moment believe that everyone who claims to be in Christ and purports to speak on behalf of Christ is telling the truth. Nor can we passively tolerate such error, thinking somehow that it is unkind, unloving, or unspiritual to confront false teaching and careless doctrine. Too much is at stake.

There is much in the Bible commanding us to be discerning, discriminating, judicious, and careful defenders of truth.[1] No single passage is more straightforward than the one I quoted above, 1 Thessalonians 5:21, 22. There Paul gives three guidelines for the discerning Christian.

JUDGE EVERYTHING

"Examine everything carefully" (v. 21) is a call to careful judgment. People are fond of quoting Matthew 7:1: "Do not judge so that you will not be judged." That verse is speaking of judging others' attitudes, motives, and the hidden things of the heart. We can't judge those things; we can't even see them. Only God can (1 Samuel 16:7). And one day He "will judge the secrets of men through Christ Jesus" (Romans 2:16). In the meantime, we are not to judge one another. In other words, we are not to condemn others' thoughts, motives, attitudes, desires, or other unseen qualities.

That does not mean, however, that we should be undiscerning. We are most certainly supposed to judge between truth and error, right and wrong, and good and evil.

Paul wrote the Corinthian church, "I speak as to wise men; you judge what I say" (1 Corinthians 10:15). Jesus said, "Judge with righteous judgment" (John 7:24). Clearly, our Lord requires us to exercise discernment, distinguishing between truth and error.

In 1 Thessalonians 5, the call to "examine everything" has particular application to preaching and teaching. Verse 20 mentions "prophetic utterances." Paul is not speaking of extrabiblical revelation, but of those whose gift was to minister the Word with prophetic authority. The modern parallel would be preaching and teaching the Word of God. "Don't despise authoritative teaching," he is saying in essence. "Rather, examine it carefully, cling to what is good, and shun the rest."

That admonition is especially timely today. It runs counter to the trends of a culture that rejects authoritative biblical exposition in favor of entertainment. It confronts the ideas of those who spurn doctrine in pursuit of "unity, " who place relationships before convictions. It challenges those who have become enamored with feelings and have lowered the value of clear thinking.

Trends like those have decimated the church. What passes for Christianity today has become far too tolerant of aberrant teaching, negligent of Scripture, and reluctant to criticize anything. Doctrinal clarity and conviction have been discarded. Discrimination and judgment have begun to sound like bad words.

In fact, many people justify their lack of discernment as charitable magnanimity toward those who differ. Thus discernment is often perceived as a malevolent attitude.

We must never be unloving, but we cannot countenance false teaching. Remember that John, the apostle of love, wrote:

> *Anyone who goes too far and does not abide in the teaching of Christ, does not have God; the one who abides in the teaching, he has both the Father and the Son. If anyone comes to you and does not bring this teaching,* do not receive him into your house, and do not give him a greeting; for the one who gives him a greeting participates in his evil deeds.
>
> —2 JOHN 9-11, EMPHASIS ADDED

We must be discerning. To be tolerant of false teaching and error is to dishonor God.

What measuring stick can we use to judge between truth and error? The Word of God. Paul was very explicit in his instructions to Timothy:

> *If anyone advocates a different doctrine and does not agree with sound words, those of our Lord Jesus Christ, and with the doctrine conforming to godliness, he is conceited and understands nothing; but he has a morbid interest in controversial questions and disputes about words, out of which arise envy, strife, abusive language, evil suspicions, and constant friction between men of depraved mind and deprived of the truth, who suppose that godliness is a means of gain.*
> —I TIMOTHY 6:3-5

The phrases "sound words, those of our Lord Jesus Christ, and . . . the doctrine conforming to godliness" refer to the body of apostolic teaching preserved for us in the New Testament. Many in Timothy's day were teaching that truth could be known intuitively (mysticism) or by some supernatural enlightenment (gnosticism). Paul was affirming that the only truth necessary for Christians was the truth revealed by God in His Word.

That's true today, though many still try to seek deeper, secret truth from other sources. There is no accurate gauge of truth besides God's Word, and we must diligently examine everything by it.

HOLD ON TO WHAT IS GOOD

"Hold fast to that which is good" is the second half of Paul's admonition in 1 Thessalonians 5:21. That echoes Romans 12:9: "Abhor what is evil; cling to what is good." It may seem like common sense for Christians to hold on to what is good. Nevertheless, Paul often repeats that same petition in his writings. As the church through the ages has so often tragically proved, it is all too easy to drop one's guard and let go of precious biblical truth. We must be diligent to defend against that.

Paul also wrote, "O Timothy, guard what has been entrusted to you" (1 Timothy 6:20). He followed that with a similar admonition in his second epistle: "Retain the standard of sound words which you have heard from me, in the faith and love which are in Christ Jesus. Guard, through the Holy Spirit who dwells in us, the treasure which has been entrusted to you" (2 Timothy 1:13, 14).

Holding fast to the truth is like guarding treasure. It requires a militant stance against any person of influence who would steal the treasure. Too many Christians have been willing to make peace with the enemies of truth, and the result has been devastating losses of the treasure of true doctrine. The Dark Ages were a bitter fruit of a church that forfeited biblical truth for the vain traditions of evil men. Early in the twentieth century many churches in Europe and North America surrendered the truth of Scripture in exchange for barren liberal theology. Time and again the people of God have failed to guard the truth—and have always paid a painful price.

We must guard the truth as a priceless treasure. Pragmatism, sensationalism, moral corruption, emotionalism, the feigned unity of ecumenism, and a host of other influences have mounted an unprecedented attack on the truth in our age. Now more than ever we need to hold fast.

Holding fast to the truth is one of the essential marks of a true Christian. The writer to the Hebrews emphasized that repeatedly: "But encourage one another day after day, as long as it is still called 'Today,' so that none of you will be hardened by the deceitfulness of sin. For we have become partakers of Christ, if we hold fast the beginning of our assurance firm until the end" (3:13, 14). Later he added, "Let us hold fast the confession of our hope without wavering, for He who promised is faithful; and let us consider how to stimulate one another to love and good deeds, not forsaking our own assembling together, as is the habit of some, but encouraging one another, and all the more as you see the day drawing near" (10:23-25).

The day *is* drawing near. The passing of time only elevates the importance of holding fast to sound doctrine. Paul told Timothy that the time would come when people would not endure sound doctrine, "but wanting to have their ears tickled, they will accumulate for themselves teachers in accordance to their own desires, and will turn away their ears from the truth and will turn aside to myths" (2 Timothy 4:3, 4). It's happening before our eyes. What is the remedy? Paul told Timothy, "Preach the word; be ready in season and out of season; reprove, rebuke, exhort, with great patience and instruction" (v. 2). We want to be found faithful.

SHUN WHAT IS EVIL

"Abstain from every form of evil" (1 Thessalonians 5:22) is the third facet of the apostle Paul's call to discernment. The word translated "abstain" is a very strong verb meaning, "hold oneself away from." It emphasizes the complete separation of the believer from evil in both teaching and behavior. When you see something that is evil, not true, and erroneous—shun it!

The word translated "evil" in this verse means "harmful, injurious, malignant." It speaks of something that is deadly poisonous. As we have seen, Paul seems to be speaking here primarily about perversions of the truth, spiritual lies, and false teaching. Of course, included in the apostle Paul's instruction would be the idea that we should shun evil moral conduct. "Abstain from every form of evil," Paul writes. Evil in any form is to be rejected. But the heart of his message is a warning against corruptions of the truth.

Nothing in Scripture gives us latitude to expose ourselves to what is not true. We are to be completely separated from all forms of evil. Does that mean Christians should be naive? In a sense, yes. The apostle Paul wrote the Romans, "I want you to be wise in what is good and innocent in what is evil" (Romans 16:19). We're not supposed to be experts about evil. Some people subscribe to the notion that the most effective way to oppose false teaching and error is to study it, master it, and then answer it. I don't believe that. We can refute false teaching far more effectively by becoming truth experts. Truth is the most powerful opponent of error, and good is the most effective adversary of evil. Paul hinted at that when he wrote, "Do not be overcome by evil, but overcome evil with good" (Romans 12:21).

When the FBI trains its agents to recognize counterfeit money, it does so by having them study the genuine article. Prospective agents spend months learning the details of how real money is engraved. Only by being intimately familiar with authentic bills can they immediately recognize the counterfeits.

So it is in the spiritual realm. Knowing and proclaiming the truth is the best way to refute error. Paul implied that when he instructed Titus on how to choose elders. An elder, Paul said, must be one who is "holding fast the faithful word which is in accordance with the teaching, so that he will be able both to exhort in sound doctrine and to refute those who contradict" (Titus 1:9). Only those who are skillful in holding forth the truth can be effective in refuting error.

Note that one of the key tasks of every elder was refuting error. That may not be in vogue in today's society, but it still is a necessary part of every spiritual leader's role. Elders must be able to refute doctrinal error so that those who lack spiritual maturity do not stumble. God has ordained this role of leadership to keep His church pure. We cannot abdicate our responsibility.

How important is discernment? Ultimately it is the definitive mark of spiritual maturity: "Solid food is for the mature, who because of practice have their senses trained to discern good and evil" (Hebrews 5:14). As you pursue spiritual growth, let the Word of God control your heart and mind, and ask the Lord to train your senses to be discerning.

Whoever is wise, let him understand these things; whoever is discerning, let him know them. For the ways of the LORD *are right, and the righteous will walk in them, but transgressors will stumble in them.*

—HOSEA 14:9

And this I pray, that your love may abound still more and more in real knowledge and all discernment.

—PHILIPPIANS 1:9

NOTES

Chapter 1
The Master Key: A Presupposition

1   For a defense of the sufficiency of Scripture, see John MacArthur, Jr.,
    Our Sufficiency in Christ (Dallas: Word Books, 1991; Wheaton, Ill.:
    Crossway Books, 1998). For a defense of the inspiration and trust-
    worthiness of the Bible, see Norman L. Geisler and William F. Nix, *A
    General Introduction to the Bible* (Chicago: Moody Press, 1986).

Chapter 4
Obedience: Unlocking the Servants' Quarters

1   See John F. MacArthur, Jr., *The Gospel According to Jesus* (Grand
    Rapids, Mich.: Zondervan, 1988) for an in-depth study of this issue.

2   "Noah's Faith, Fear, Obedience, and Salvation," in *The Metropolitan
    Tabernacle Pulpit* (1890; Pasadena, Tex.: Pilgrim Publications, 1974
    reprint), 36:303.

Chapter 5
The Filling of the Spirit: Unlocking the Power Plant

1   John MacArthur, Jr., *Found: God's Will* (Wheaton, Ill.: Victor Books,
    1977), pp. 21, 22.

Chapter 8
Prayer: Unlocking the Inner Sanctum

1   For a complete treatment of the Christian's spiritual sufficiency, see
    John MacArthur, Jr., *Our Sufficiency in Christ* (Dallas: Word Books,
    1991; Wheaton, Ill.: Crossway Books, 1998).

Chapter 11
Fellowship: Unlocking the Family Room

1   Millard J. Erickson, *Concise Dictionary of Christian Theology* (Grand
    Rapids, Mich.: Baker, 1986), p. 140.

2   Walter E. Elwell, ed., *Baker Encyclopedia of the Bible* (Grand Rapids,
    Mich.: Baker, 1988), 2:1252.

3   Louis Berkhof, *Systematic Theology* (Grand Rapids, Mich.: William B.
    Eerdmans, 1981), p. 469.

4   For a discussion of spiritual gifts, see John F. MacArthur, Jr., *The Charismatic Chaos* (Grand Rapids, Mich.: Zondervan Publishing House, 1992).

Chapter 12
Witnessing: Unlocking the Nursery

1   Gene A. Getz, *Sharpening the Focus of the Church* (Chicago: Moody Press, 1974), p. 41.

2   For additional discussion on this and other issues related to evangelism, see John F. MacArthur, *Nothing but the Truth* (Wheaton, Ill.: Crossway Books, 1999), especially pp. 147-169.

Chapter 13
Discernment: Locking the Security Gate

1   For a thorough study of the subject of discernment, see John F. MacArthur, *Reckless Faith* (Wheaton, Ill.: Crossway Books, 1994).

Scripture Index

GENERAL INDEX